MY YEAR AS A CRUISE SHIP DOCTOR

UP YOUR GAME

DR PAOLO AMODEO

Up Your Game
© Dr Paolo Amodeo 2022

All rights reserved. No part of this publication may be reproduced, stored in a retrieval system, or transmitted in any form or by any means, electronic, mechanical, photocopying, recording or otherwise, without the prior written permission of the author.

ISBN: 978-1-922854-77-3 (Paperback)
         978-1-922854-78-0 (eBook)

A catalogue record for this book is available from the National Library of Australia

Editors: Chloe Cran
Cover Design: Ocean Reeve Publishing
Design and Typeset: Ocean Reeve Publishing
Printed in Australia by Ocean Reeve Publishing

Published by Dr Paolo Amodeo and Ocean Reeve Publishing
www.oceanreevepublishing.com

Ocean
REEVE
PUBLISHING

To my wonderful wife and kids: Kaz, Sofia, Luca, and Sacha.

And in remembrance of the late great Dr Mo.

This is a true story, and 99% of all the events and incidents are completely real. (See if you can guess which tiny insignificant occurrence is the only one that is made up!)

To respect the privacy of some of the characters who might not wish to be recognised, I have changed some names and details to enable this.

CONTENTS

1. Dr Mo and the Bates Street Boys 1
2. Vomit 13
3. Mr D and the Cocaine Shooter 25
4. Captain's Cock 37
5. Illegal Aliens and the Balls of Fire 55
6. The Great Escape 69
7. Spinal Tap and the Cuban Muscle Crisis 79
8. The Devil and the Deep Blue Sea 97
9. Going Down 109
10. Alabama Slammer 127
11. Back to Basics 141
12. Men of Mystery 153

1

DR MO AND THE BATES STREET BOYS

Dr Mo scurried into the hotel lobby like a ferret on speed. As he approached, it was impossible not to notice his odd appearance. Standing five foot five and slight of frame, his untidy, jet-black quiff towered above his head. With a perfectly matching stick-on moustache, brown fuck-off shirt collars, and agonisingly short fawn slacks, Carnival Cruise Line's medical director was a dead ringer for a 1970s streetwise undercover TV cop. He even sported the obligatory cigarette in hand, from which he inhaled deeply at worryingly short intervals.

Dirk and I had already spoken to our new boss several times over long-distance telephone calls, but we remained apprehensive about meeting him for the first time. His gently persuasive tone combined with his Mexican bandit accent made him sound a little quirky, perhaps even eccentric, which only added to the enigmatic picture we had of him.

And what sort of name was Doctor Mo, anyway?

'Hel-lo boys,' sleazed Mo, shaking our hands in turn.

'Dirk. Pao-lo. Welcome to Miami. Nice to finally meet you! You must be tired after your flight from London. But we've got to catch the next flight to Orlando straight away. The minibus will take us from there to Port Canaveral, where the ships will be waiting for you.'

'Paolo, Guy will meet you on the *Carnivale* and give you a handover before he leaves for the *Tropicale*. Dirk, you're on the *Mardi Gras*. Your friend Pete's currently at sea on the *Celebration*. He's very happy there! You know, you two are lucky to have such good friends like Pete and Guy. They told me so many wonderful things about you both, I couldn't wait to get you on the ships too!'

It was an extraordinary turn of events. Friends since medical school, the four of us would now be simultaneously zig-zagging our way across the Caribbean as Carnival Cruise Line's first ever British doctors. We were twenty-five years old. But there wasn't a moment to reflect on the cavalier yearbook ambition that started it all.

'Oh my God, look at the time! We have to run for the plane,' declared Mo, lighting another cigarette.

Airborne on the way to Orlando, our new boss was certainly in full flight. Barely pausing for breath, Dr Mo smoked a whole packet of cigarettes while chatting up all the air hostesses and simultaneously explaining everything we needed to know about being cruise ship doctors.

'Before you sail, check the manifest for passengers with complex histories—wise to be prepared. If you're going to do any surgery, try to avoid high seas. I've performed a million haemorrhoidectomies!

'As the ship's physician, you read every crew member's health records and therefore know all their sensitive medical information. This gives you great professional power to make decisions about fitness for work, organise hospitalisation in port, and order evacuations at sea—decisions that not even the captain is qualified to make or overrule.

'And the doctor is the only person onboard with the power to diagnose the captain as clinically insane and unfit for duty!'

Dirk and I looked at each other incredulously.

'Yes, you have tremendous authority,' Mo continued. 'Some of your patients will become your friends, maybe even your girlfriends. Learn true or false motives quickly; some staff will be needing favours, and others are there to guarantee you don't upset the status quo.'

It was clear that behind the sartorial and cigarette smokescreen was a remarkable character with an uncanny ability to read people and complex situations. We liked him immediately. Mo lit another cigarette before delivering his pièce de résistance: a parable about power, privilege, and hierarchy derived from the decade he'd spent climbing the ladder from ship's doctor to medical director for one of the world's largest cruise lines.

'You must play The Game. You see, I have worked on these ships for many years, and I know what kind of people you will be dealing with. Make friends with the chief of security at your first opportunity. Slip your room steward something when you get paid. The captain always tries to surround himself with friends and loyal officers. If you don't agree with the captain, don't tell him, tell me. He likes quiet, well-behaved crew. The Captain's Mob will see your unique power as a threat and will view you with enormous suspicion until proven otherwise.'

He lit another cigarette before shifting his eagle-eye from the hostess to Dirk. Tall, slim and permanently tanned, with blonde locks and a big nose, Dirk was Sheffield's very own version of Barry Manilow. Women saw his captivating charm and overt sexuality as utterly irresistible. Music and passion were always his fashion, and he never failed to exploit it.

'Oh my God, I can see now that I'm going to have trouble with you! Stay away from the passengers—you can screw the crew as much as you like, but don't let the Italians know; they get very jealous. For sure, have a great time, party, meet lots of women, but don't forget ship's doctors are their main target. All American mothers tell their daughters to marry a doctor. So be careful. And remember who is the boss. The captain is the most powerful person on the ship. If he is after a certain woman that maybe you like also, let him carry on. There will be many others. Be discreet. Trust no-one.'

Dirk rubbed his hands with glee, convinced that the Caribbean and its cruise lines were made exclusively to accommodate his Copacabana good looks.

'Paolo, I'm certain you can be just as wild, given the chance, but don't let people take advantage of your good nature. Thank God you seem more steady,' Mo noted, right on target. 'Some people will want to see you both slip up. Be careful, and take a little time to find out how things work and who you can trust. I can see something in you guys, and

I know you will enjoy this lifestyle just like Pete and Guy. They are both doing very well. I think that you two will do even better and be the best doctors we've ever had!'

It seemed like skilful flattery, but Dr Mo was also basking in the glory of his recruitment triumph.

In charge of hiring and firing, Dr Mo encountered recurring problems attracting and keeping American doctors. They struggled with the ships' basically equipped infirmaries, demanded high wages, and didn't necessarily view the neighbouring Caribbean as a particularly glamorous travel opportunity. Casting his net further only proved that Central American doctors didn't have a good track record. He began to wonder if doctors from the UK's great and well-respected National Health Service (NHS) might be better suited to meet the demands of medical practice onboard a cruise ship. It turned out to be quite an astute assumption.

As a publicly funded healthcare system, the NHS offered free and comprehensive services to 50 million British citizens and, as such, lacked the lavish resources of US private medicine. Unlike our American counterparts, there could be no over-reliance on expensive tests and technologies, and it was ingrained into our mindset that we should only order tests that were deemed absolutely essential. Plus, in the US, patients were far more likely to sue their doctor, resulting in the widespread practice of defensive medicine, defined by ordering every test under the sun.

British undergraduate training was far more clinical in nature, with an emphasis on taking a good history and physical examination in order to arrive at a diagnosis.

UK doctors were also well versed in the concept of 'masterly inactivity', an important clinical skill passed down the generations. The idea is that many things are minor and get better on their own, and over-investigating and over-treating can often lead to a worse outcome. Sometimes it's better to take a step back and simply observe. The key to masterly inactivity is accurately recognising in a timely manner exactly when intervention *might* be required.

This is the essence of the art of medicine, which I embraced wholeheartedly during my training. Indeed, the motto of the one-hundred-and-sixty-year-old Sheffield University Medical School that we all attended served to underwrite the fact that our profession is more than just the practice of scientific knowledge:

Ars Longa Vita Brevis. Art is Long, Life is Short.

As the plane began its descent, I realised that the sparkling, dazzling Caribbean was a million miles from the rain-soaked, grimy Yorkshire steel towns from which the seeds of our friendship had sprung. And we had travelled a long and winding road which led us to exotic Miami and the magnificent Dr Mo.

I had first met Dirk on a fourth-year student secondment to Scunthorpe Hospital, forty miles east of Sheffield, in late 1988. I'd always seen him around medical school in the preceding few years, but we hardly knew each other. But all that changed after a Friday night trip from Sunny Scunny back to Sheffield with Dirk and his current muse, a Scottish occupational therapist called Lucy. It involved one fast car, a pepperoni pizza, and a bottle of Johnny Walker Black Label and ended in a dramatic crash into a police Range Rover. Our car ended up in a ditch. However, my negative breathalyser test kept me out of jail and helped to relax the cops, who happily joined the party, sharing our pizza to the tune of The Cult's 'She Sells Sanctuary' still blaring out from my car stereo.

This high-speed collision ignited an immediate and intense bond between polar opposites: Dirk, the flamboyant extrovert, and me, the quiet introvert.

It also sparked the creation of the notorious Bates Street Boys after Dirk and I soon teamed up with two like-minded contemporaries, Pete and Guy. The four of us established a rock-solid fellowship as we managed the difficult transition from students to junior doctors in Sheffield.

Yorkshire was certainly no Garden of Eden, but we were determined to taste the forbidden fruits that life had to offer.

In April 1990, the four of us took a holiday to the Greek island of Kos, home to Hippocrates. Did we visit his famous monument and the ancient tree under which the Father of Medicine taught his pupils?

No, we invented the Kos Kocktail. This comprised a mix of drugs taken before we hit the bottle on our nights out: a prochlorperazine (anti-nausea), a ranitidine (anti-acid), and a doxycycline (anti-STI antibiotic). All washed down with a big glass of ouzo.

Shortly after our Greek odyssey, the four of us moved into a shared house together on Bates Street in Sheffield, not far from our old university. This deepened our endeavours to take the world by storm, and we set the tone with a legendary November 5th Guy Fawkes Bonfire Night party.

All was going swimmingly until Guy decided to emulate his 17th-century namesake with his very own Gunpowder Plot. This DIY fireworks display climaxed in a spur-of-the-moment effort to incinerate twenty of our innocent guests. Seeing a tightly packed rabble on the small garden terrace, all clutching cans of Special Brew and half-baked potatoes, the trainee surgeon calmly lobbed a sizzling rocket into the crowd while repeatedly headbutting a frying pan. Inevitably, panic ensued, but fortunately the only casualty was the kitchen door, which suffered extensive third-degree burns and was pronounced dead at the scene.

Five years later, a friend and year of '89 classmate, Stevie B, told us how a junior colleague recounted the story of a wild bonfire night party where the house got pretty well trashed and the kitchen door cremated. The irony was not lost on Steve, who had in fact been the owner of 56 Bates Street when the party took place. While he had been none too chuffed at the resulting carnage, a different landlord might have seen Guy hung, drawn, and quartered.

On any given night during those formative years in Sheffield, the four of us would invariably meet up at 3 am at Napoleon's Casino, a small private club over the west side of town, comparing stories. Dirk's exploits always revolved around the evening's conquest and a quick trip back to his place. Pete, aka Lawsy, would have a story of derring-do that typically involved scaling a fifteen-foot wall and braving barbed wire and broken glass to visit a girlfriend in the nurses' residence, only to break into the wrong room and be thrown out by security.

As for me, I generally left the more boisterous behaviour to the others. I would have spent an hour asleep on the comfy sofa at some local dive before waking up to the sound of good music and dancing my way through four different nightclubs on the way to our casino rendezvous.

I was never the most dynamic of people, and I always looked to do things with the minimum of fuss—there was no point in wasting precious energy on small talk, animated facial expressions, or propensities to flap about like headless chickens in the face of a medical emergency. In fact, I've always been guided by one of the most fundamental laws of physics—the first law of thermodynamics: the total energy of an isolated system is constant, and energy can be neither created nor destroyed. This is also known as the law of conservation of energy, and for a person of limited energy like me, it's a great excuse for a siesta.

Overcoming my extreme shyness was my biggest personal and professional challenge. My quiet and unassertive nature made me feel a little out of place amongst the many Type A personalities in the world of acute hospital medicine. I classed my personality as Type Z. Talking was not my thing, and I found it very stressful meeting new people, which of course included my patients. Even in the company of my closest friends, there would often be no words entering my conscious brain to deliver to my mouth. After a particularly quiet evening on my part, Guy once asked me in a light-hearted manner, 'Paolo, are you a manic-depressive or something?'

'No, I'm a depressive-depressive.'

At least I never missed the opportunity to crack a joke.

Although various six-month postings across regional hospitals saw us move in and out of each other's orbits, we all continued to exert a strong influence on the lives of our fellow Bates Street Boys. But it was Guy's defiant, indomitable decision to kill a flock of birds with one lion-hearted stone that had the most magnetic effect on us all.

Despite wanting to be a surgeon, Guy had always eschewed the norm: school, medical school, surgical career, retirement. By 1991, he was at the crossroad. Upcoming surgical exams and a study load to rival his debts would perpetuate the predictable journey. Guy opted for enlightenment, which he sought by carpet-bombing ads for overseas postings in the British Medical Journal: the American Hospital in Paris, the British Antarctic Expedition, a few jobs in outback Australia, and a Miami-based cruise company called Carnival.

Pete was on exactly the same path, searching for anything that would afford him a year's adventurous sabbatical and a high-paying job that would clear his phenomenal debts and leave him time to study before jumping back on the surgical conveyor belt.

They both held four aces: six months of emergency medicine, excellent timing, chutzpah, and a belief that the first response would be destiny's choice.

Carnival was the first to reply.

Shortly after their interviews in London, Dr Mo called and asked if they could start urgently, in a mere three weeks' time. So, on the 8th of August 1991, Guy, dressed in his best shoulder-padded suit, with slip-on lavender-coloured shoes to compliment his jacket lining, headed for Heathrow Airport with Pete, who wore a matching certainty that their distinguished and superior medical talents lay behind Mo's quick and eager response.

Only later did they learn that one of Carnival's onboard medics had been found in his cabin with fifty-four empty bottles of vodka, creating an instant job vacancy that needed filling *tout de suite*.

When Pete and Guy arrived at Miami International airport, they felt the blast of ninety-degree heat for the first time in their lives. And who knows, without their slice of timely good fortune, the Bates Street Boys could have ended up spending the next twelve months freezing our arses off in the South Pole.

A few months later, Dirk and I realised we held a similar hand. I was currently in an emergency medicine job in Bristol and had recently passed my primary surgical exams, which meant I had something tangible under my belt for when I returned. Taking a year out from surgical training to work in the Caribbean was certainly a career risk; the traditionally minded surgeons in charge of my future employment would surely view it with disdain. But like Pete and Guy, I knew exactly what lay before me: hard work, long hours, more exams, and a career in which there was no turning back. None of that put me off surgery, but it fired a determination to expand my horizons and open myself up to the wider world.

The stars were aligned. The opportunity for adventure might never come again, and the excitement of not knowing what was around the corner was a real thrill. Dirk agreed.

So, in March 1992, we completed our long journey from Sunny Scunny to the Sunshine State and touched down at Miami airport, ready to meet Dr Mo. We had arrived.

2
VOMIT

'I've left you the essentials: a dozen bottles of booze and five hundred cigarettes. Your cabin has a double bed and ensuite bathroom, which for this old tug is the lap of luxury. You can keep my TV and video player. Oh, and watch out for the toilet, Paolo—it has a nasty habit of vomiting at you!'

'Wow, you've left me an entire pub! Nice one, Guy.'

'That's one of the perks of being the ship's doctor. All senior officers have a weekly allowance of one bottle of spirits and two hundred cigarettes.'

'Really?'

'Yeah, apparently it goes back to the old days of sailors' rum rations.'

Yo ho ho, and a bottle of rum!

I could hardly have expected any different kind of welcome from Guy. His generosity, intelligence, wit, and sometimes feverish eloquence made him excellent company, which I had missed since he had left the UK. Guy's outspoken nature and tendency for bizarre drunken behaviour had become legendary in Sheffield Medical School, where his career ambition was recorded in our Year of '89 Yearbook: *To imbibe, inhale, ingest and impale; and to inanely indulge.*

But the literal pursuit of his yearbook ambition had proved expensive. Guy's over-indulgence had climbed steadily during his five years in medical school, and by two years post-graduation, his mountain of debt far exceeded his annual salary. For a junior doctor working up to a hundred hours a week on a meagre wage in the publicly funded UK healthcare system, it had become an insurmountable Everest. So, Guy did what any broke, overworked trainee surgeon living in freezing cold South Yorkshire would do: he wrangled a well-paid, more laid-back and tax-free job in the Caribbean as Carnival Cruise Line's first ever UK-trained ship's doctor. At the extraordinarily tender age of twenty-five, Guy was now seventh in command of a Carnival 'Fun Ship', attending to the medical needs of five hundred crew members and a thousand passengers intent on having the most riotous fun possible.

And in just a few moments, he would be passing that mantle over to me.

I had followed Guy's audacious leap from the UK to the tropics, attracted by the allure of sun, sand, and, of course, sea. My naïve expectation was that Guy should now resemble a well-tanned character from *Miami Vice*. But, true to form, it was clear that his stint on the high seas had been less Miami, more Vice, as the only detectable change since we had last met was the ashen appearance of both his hair and his complexion. In his younger days, Guy's greyness was somewhat of a curiosity, but now the silver mop was undoubtedly his most striking feature. Combined with his ghostly countenance and all-white officer's uniform, he now looked like a white-washed albino after a visit by the local vampire.

'So, Guy, how come you look so pale after you've just spent half a year in the Caribbean?'

'I've spent the last few months in bed, sleeping off a hangover, wanking, and playing Nintendo. After you've been to the Bahamas twice a week for six months, the novelty kind of wears off. So, I've reached Level 53 on Sim City, probably need a liver transplant, and have a right forearm like Popeye!'

Notwithstanding Guy's tendency for exaggeration, I found all this rather difficult to believe. Everybody knows there are only thirty levels in Sim City.

The tss (twin-screw steamship) *Carnivale*, the cruise liner that was to be my home for the next six months, was built in a Scottish shipyard in 1956 and originally named the *Empress of Britain*. The 31,000-tonne vessel had started off as a transatlantic liner before it was bought by Carnival in the mid-1970s, becoming the second of the 'Fun Ship' fleet to sail the Caribbean from its new base in Florida. By 1991, it had been relegated to short cruises from Port Canaveral to the Bahamas, leaving the longer and more glamorous Caribbean itineraries to the modern state-of-the-art super-liners.

But despite its shabby interiors, general decrepitude, and old-fashioned Stephenson Rocket engineering, the *Carnivale* did have one advantage over the newer ships; it was safer, on account of its deep hull. The modern vessels were largely flat bottomed, and more unstable as a result. On its test launch in 1987, the brand-new super-liner ms (motor ship) *Celebration* had lurched alarmingly to starboard, so an enormous concrete log counterbalance was welded onto its port-side hull.

Guy explained our next move. 'Paolo, we don't have long before the ship sets sail. So, I'll give you a quick tour before I have to get off.'

We left my new quarters, turning down the narrow corridor that immediately led to a heavy steel door marked *Crew Only*. This conveniently opened into the crew bar, a rather ramshackle affair encompassing a small, windswept portion of the aft deck in which was strewn half a dozen weather-beaten plastic tables and chairs. Cheap beer and cocktails were sold from a small, flaking wooden booth adorned with an old, faded Tina Turner poster and staffed by Jorge, the most miserable barman on the high seas.

Guy explained the importance of this small area of the ship.

'This is the only place of recreation for the crew who work in the galley or engine room, or some other godforsaken hole. And most of those poor bastards work up to sixteen hours a day. Only officers and staff such as pursers, casino croupiers, gift shop assistants, and entertainers are allowed in the passenger areas while off duty.'

The crew bar was a colourful and noisy place. A constant, irritating backbeat of loud salsa crackled over the cheap stereo system, intermittently drowned out by the catastrophic crash of a Jamaican busboy slamming his domino piece onto the table as though an act of war. Then a Haitian cabin steward was accused of palming the double-six, launching him into a frenzied stream of patois, complete with the demonic voodoo eyes of a man possessed.

I was rather taken aback, as it looked like a fight was about to break out within ten minutes of me boarding the ship!

But Guy explained that this was just normal behaviour for the crew bar.

'There's rarely any real trouble here. Some of the Italian officers always lurk around in the bar, which prevents things from escalating. The junior stripes always keep half an eye on their subordinates, but mostly they're here for a sneaky leer at the nubile young dancers popping in for a few cheap rum and cokes in between shows.'

But there was no time for a drink on Guy's lightning tour. After high-fiving Jorge and half of the Caribbean calypso band, we headed below deck.

'I'll show you some of the crew quarters—it will give you an idea of the tough conditions they live in.'

We briskly spiralled down a dozen metal-frame staircases, weaving through the spartan steel warren of the crew quarters, dodging angular stairwells and ducking under makeshift clothes lines until we reached the windowless Deck Three. Semi-naked men of all shapes and colours gripped toilet bags and waited patiently by the showers.

Guy introduced me to one of the crew in the line-up.

'Ah, Salvadore, ¿como estas?'

'*Soy bueno,* Dr Guy. Sorry to see you leaving!'

'Paolo, this is Salvadore Martinez. He's one of the onboard carpenters. But you know what? He's also an orthopaedic surgeon in Costa Rica!'

We shook hands, his double professional skills manifesting in a very muscular, vice-like grip.

'Wow, that's pretty cool!' I smiled, politely ignoring the effect of the friendly, bone-crushing procedure.

Guy waved the senior surgeon farewell as we continued on.

'*Adios amigo!*'

'You know, Salvadore has helped me out a few times when I needed some advice on orthopaedic cases. Of course, his input was unofficial, so his fee was a crate of beer!'

'So how did he end up here as a carpenter?'

'He told me he had some family problems and needed cash to help sort it out. Apparently screwing a few rivets on a ship pays more than screwing a few hips in Costa Rica.'

The corridor filled with steam escaping from the hot laundry, along with the unmistakable stench of boiled cabbage. A bit further on, we passed by the Korean kitchen, emanating its aroma of simmering, sweaty socks. We turned sharp left, then right, through two more heavy fire doors, then right again.

'And this is Mr Kim's cabin,' declared Guy as he gestured for me to take a peek inside.

I gingerly looked into what amounted to a large cupboard to find a smiling Oriental man of indiscriminate age greeting me eagerly. I shook his hand as I looked around the tiny room and saw a small single bed and a bedside table piled high with bits of paper, receipt books, and a cash box. The only other contents of this man's cabin were hundreds and hundreds of video tapes hugging the walls from floor to ceiling, all neatly indexed, perfectly aligned and grouped by category. There was everything from horror films to westerns to comedies, but the biggest collections by far were porn films and martial art movies.

Guy explained what lay before us.

'Mr Kim officially runs the ship's laundry with the Korean boys. But his video rental sideline is far more lucrative—he's put his two sons through college on the profits! He also runs his own dry-cleaning service and does suit alterations on request. No-one's ever seen him sleep.'

Mr Kim's eyes lit up as he laughed, probably in anticipation of my badly fitting standard-issue uniform and penchant for kung-fu porno films.

'Plus, if you need any cheap electronic goods, CDs, or computer stuff, then Mr Kim is The Man.'

We bade Mr Kim farewell and made our way towards the engine room. Deeper we went, descending through a series of smaller and smaller steel hatches and ever-decreasing circles of narrowing stairwells. Soon it was difficult to stand upright or securely place a foot on the tiny steps. The next steel hatch opened to a sudden wall of heat so intense that it took my breath away. We ducked inside and emerged onto a narrow metal gantry overlooking the engine room, the pumping heart of the vessel. Heat and steam and oil and noise flooded the senses. I observed the team of hot, ruddy men about to burst in a sea of sweat, turning heavy brass wheels and adjusting dials on ungainly consoles. Pistons pumped and hoses hissed and valves vibrated in a fearsome cacophony.

Just passing through Hell, I thought. Any minute now, we'll be accosted by a horned underling of Satan, prodding us with his red-hot trident and putting us to work shovelling coal into the furnace for all eternity.

'Hey!' A loud, gruff voice reverberated around the steel interior.

Startled, I quickly spun around to be greeted by a portly Italian engineer wearing grubby blue overalls and a startling collection of chunky gold jewellery. Smiling broadly, his sparkling gold teeth glittered through the grease and grime. I politely shook his oily hand.

'Piacere, signore!' I shouted above the din of Dante's Inferno.

'This is Sanfilippo!' bellowed Guy. 'He's a great man!'

Guy and the bejewelled engineer shared a warm hug of farewell.

'Looks like they're cranking up the engines. You'll be sailing soon. I'll introduce you to the captain before I get off.'

It was a hard, steady climb back up to the main deck, and on our way, we met a constant stream of people eager to wish Guy a fond farewell—he was obviously well liked by many of the crew below deck.

'So, what's the deal with Sanfilippo?' I ventured, as clearly, he wasn't just one of Dante's regular engine-room mob.

'Ah.' Guy leant over and checked around us as he explained their relationship sotto-voce.

'Sanfilippo is the king down here. But he has a chronic heart condition—mild cardiac failure. It doesn't cause too much of a problem, but he doesn't want Carnival to know.'

'Really?'

'Yeah. The thing is, if the company finds out, he'll get fired.'

'Hmm, that sounds a bit dodgy.'

'Well, maybe. But things work a bit differently around here. Sanfilippo is very well connected, especially in Nassau. If you treat him well, he can get you free restaurant vouchers at the casinos, and a whole heap of other stuff.'

It was becoming rapidly apparent that in this region of the ship lurked an underworld ghetto with its own unwritten rules and codes of conduct, and Sanfilippo was obviously more than just another grubby boiler suit. The unofficial hierarchy aboard ship clearly had its own organised web of tentacles and, indeed, *omertà*.

This was crucial knowledge for a fresh-faced and naïve senior officer-to-be.

Having clambered our way back up from the bowels of the ship, we eventually hit fresh air and blue skies. We took a moment to catch our breath. Guy explained that although Carnival was an American company, each ship was navigated by Italians and registered in Africa (Liberia, usually) or Panama. And now medically staffed by Brits!

'The engineers and officers on the bridge are all Italian. Most are alright, but some will treat you with suspicion, and …'

A tall, white-haired gentleman in a dazzling officer's uniform loomed ominously into view, stopping us in our tracks.

'Captain Fornari! This is my good friend Paolo Amodeo. He'll be taking over from me as of today.'

The Master's deep dark eyes and craggy features lightened somewhat. *'Ah ... paesano! Sei Italiano allora?'*

Excellent, I thought, *this will put me straight into his good books,* as I replied in perfect Italian. *'Si ... er ...'*

'Da dove?' enquired the captain.

'Sicilia,' I replied. I was now on a roll. Maybe even a cannolo. *'Sono nato in Galles, pero mio padre é Siciliano.'*

Captain Fornari frowned and pensively rubbed his chin. 'Hmm, Sicily ...' he repeated. 'I am from Genova. We will talk later; now I must take charge on the bridge.'

He then departed, huffing and puffing, muttering to himself. Guy had remained silent during this brief exchange, then spoke to me through gritted teeth.

'Ah. One thing I forgot to mention. The Sicilians and the Genovese have a longstanding feud. They hate each other. Shit. Sorry.'

'Thanks, Guy.'

He doubled up as I affectionately winded him with my elbow.

'Look, Paolo, I've run out of time to show you the infirmary. It's on the aft upper deck, on the port side. I've got to get off now. I start on the *Tropicale* tomorrow!'

And with that, he quickly departed.

Vomit

Now then, I pondered. Port is the left-hand side of the ship, but I'm facing backwards. So … what was the front bit called? Shit, I'm lost already.

The floor began to move, and I realised we were away.

I must find the infirmary, I thought. I wandered aimlessly around my new home but was getting more disorientated with each turn, bumping into coachloads of newly arrived passengers trying to balance their welcome-aboard 'Fun Ship Special' cocktails and looking for their first feed of the cruise.

As the ship lurched out of port, I felt the first wave of nausea. *Must. Find. The. Infirmary.*

Tripping over odd pieces of luggage strategically positioned along the narrow corridors, I tried to stagger my way to the infirmary. But this proved to be no easy task, as the ship's medical department turned out to be both tiny and well hidden, deep in the rabbit-warren of claustrophobic decks and hallways. Eventually, aided by the trail of deck pizzas strewn along the ship by similarly nauseated new arrivals, I found the haven I'd been seeking. A queue of noisy Hawaiian shirts had accumulated near the infirmary door, looking for anti-seasickness pills. I clambered past them all one by one, clinging to the wall and stepping on toes. The initial look of disdain on their faces changed to one of horror as suddenly my colour drained and I broke out in a sweat.

'Next!' announced the nurse wearily from the small doorway. The look on her face betrayed her reluctance to see yet another spewing newcomer. Her slight scowl then quickly transformed into the wrath of a gorgon as my liquid, orange projectile splattered her pristine white outfit squarely in the midriff.

'Oh, Jesus!' she squirmed. 'That's all I need. First the new doctor doesn't show up, and now I get friggin' puked on!'

I reached out and grabbed the doorframe to steady myself, wiped the strings of vomit from my chin, and sheepishly announced, 'Hello … I'm Doctor Amodeo. The new ship's physician.'

3

MR D AND THE COCAINE SHOOTER

Once I had settled in onboard the *Carnivale*, it became apparent that I could live a fantasy life of relative luxury if I played my cards right, a million miles from the rain-soaked, intense working week back in the UK. As a senior officer, I would be entitled to many perks. Only officers had cabins of their own, staff and crew having to share rooms and toilets. I would have my own cabin steward to clean my room, take my laundry, run errands, and do any other odd jobs if suitably looked after. I would enjoy waiter service in the officers' mess, and on occasion dine at the captain's table in the passengers' dining room. All the facilities on the ship—swimming pools, sun decks, bars, gym, and all the shows were at my disposal except for the casino, which was strictly off limits (and probably just as well).

I decided it would be wise to heed Mo's advice and keep a reasonably low profile for the first month or so until I gained people's confidence and respect. Fortunately, this didn't prove too difficult a task. My daily routine largely involved relaxing in the sun reading a suitably intellectual novel, like

Gabriel Garcia Marquez's masterpiece *Love in the Time of Cholera*, and seeing the occasional patient with sunburn by day, while sipping a few quiet drinks at the shows in the evening before retiring early. This easily convinced those who mattered of my quiet and studious nature.

The light workload aboard ship gave me a chance to relax for the first time in ages. My first few weeks were still well spent, quietly observing the social mechanics and politics of this bizarre new living environment. I remembered Mo's words: 'Trust no-one and play The Game.'

Who would be useful people to know? Who should I be wary of, and who could I trust? And who was the local gossip?

It was no secret that Captain Fornari had not liked Guy and took a dim view of any unseemly behaviour. He had been Master of the tss *Carnivale* for years and saw it as his property, his home. The seafaring veteran was an old-fashioned and inflexible individual.

Every captain would have his own henchmen and informants who would dutifully report back on new personnel and potential troublemakers. These agents of doom were usually a couple of sleazy junior Italian officers eager to please their master in return for a whiff of power or a dog biscuit. Often found lurking together, comparing gold jewellery or discussing the attributes of the new Swedish croupier, this pair of lounge lizards would invariably end up in the disco, desperately chatting up a couple of old warthogs previously untouched by human bargepole.

Their other mission, of course, was to report on dubious activities, drunkenness, dangerous liaisons, or any gossip they could lay their grubby little hands on. Although these shady characters were easy to spot, the master would have a network of more covert agents in his employ—the eager young dancer who may care to gain his favour, an overworked junior purser looking for a fast-track to early promotion, or an assistant bar manager bearing a grudge against his demanding boss. With all these potential spies, plus the semi-comatose security guards, very little that took place aboard ship went unnoticed, even if relayed solely in the name of gossip.

In contrast, when docked in port, much of the crew were free to disembark and do as they please. There would be the usual hangouts where the same old faces would congregate, but in most ports, it was possible to go off the beaten track, exploring different beaches, bars, and restaurants without too much effort.

The main problem then was in getting back to the ship in time to sail in one piece and with an air of apparent sobriety.

The *Carnivale* and *Mardi Gras* shared the same itinerary of one three-day, then one four-day cruise to Nassau, so twice per week, Dirk and I would get out and about. Once the ship was docked, if anyone got sick, the local medical services would be called, and so we were off the hook for the day. The usual crew hangout in Nassau was Goombay Beach Club. Situated on a beach just a few miles down the road from the harbour, it hosted a late-night party that included live local calypso bands.

Both ships were due to set sail at 5 am, and the duty officers on the bridge always got a little nervous as this sailing time approached. Dirk and I would usually stagger out of a cab and onto the pier at 4.55 am, at which point the gangway guard would inform the relieved officer of our impending embarkation onto our respective ships.

The Captain's Meeting took place at nine o'clock the following morning, as if purposefully arranged to survey the damage incurred by Nassau Nights on his senior officers. This occurred once every cruise, and each department head would impart relevant information or report any problems suitable for open discussion. This usually involved statements of sales and profits during the previous cruise from the casino, bars, bingo, and excursions. My job was to report on any serious medical cases, drink gallons of coffee, and look green.

There was also the case of the mysterious 'Mr D', about whom the captain enquired at my first meeting.

'So, Dr Amodeo. What about Mr D?' asked Captain Fornari in his dour manner.

Who is he talking about? I wondered.

Horrified that I may have been ashore or otherwise indisposed when some ghastly near-death experience befell the poor 'Mr D', I nonchalantly spilled my coffee and murmured, 'Um … he's fine.'

Hoping that I may have gotten away with it, I wasn't sure which reaction unnerved me most: the muffled guffaws from the Food & Beverage (F&B) and Casino Managers or the mournful look of pity on the face of Captain Fornari.

After an agonising pause, the identity of Mr D was eventually revealed by the Staff Captain, the ship's second-in-command. Much to my relief, and unending amusement, 'Mr D' was merely a cleverly disguised codename for the word 'diarrhoea'. The master obviously could not stomach to utter the most revolting word in the entire English language. So, it was now clear that as the highly qualified ship's physician, it was my duty to report on the number of cases of runny bottoms presenting over the previous week.

Even though I was only a trainee surgeon at this time, I still found it strange being referred to as a 'physician'.

There has always been a friendly rivalry between physicians and surgeons, largely due to their differing skills and mindsets. Traditionally, physicians are the nerdy academic boffins, whereas surgeons are viewed as Neanderthal manual labourers, partly due to their distant origins as barbers. Closing elevator doors could be stopped by the hands of a physician. A surgeon, however, would use his head.

A classic apocryphal tale of battle between physicians and surgeons has them pitted against each other on a lengthy pub crawl. The first team who showed weakness by having to take a piss would be deemed the loser. The physicians brought with them a pharmaceutical masterplan that they thought unbeatable. They each took a sniff of DDAVP, a drug based on a natural hormone that would greatly reduce urine production. However, several pubs and many beers later, the physicians were dumbfounded when they eventually had to pee and concede defeat to their arch rivals. How could this be?

The fact was, the surgeons had each catheterised themselves beforehand and worn urine-collecting leg-bags concealed under their trousers, enabling their incredible victory.

No doubt such a disappointing defeat must have been the inspiration for a classic physician's joke describing a surgical counterpart:

What is the definition of a sigmoidoscope?
A metal tube with an arsehole at either end.

I soon understood how seeing only a couple of patients per day had caused Guy to get quite bored after a few months on the *Carnivale*. The contrast with my previous jobs in the good old NHS was striking.

UK doctors began their careers as house officers on the lowest rung of the professional ladder in hospitals across the country. Some of the more senior doctors loved calling us 'house dogs'. The workload was staggering, and many house jobs encompassed a working week somewhere between eighty and one hundred hours. Surviving and, indeed, thriving in these junior doctor roles felt like being forged in fire.

On top of assessing all new patient admissions, it was a house dog's duty to take all the blood tests, put in every intravenous cannula, and mix all the antibiotics, in addition to the mind-numbing amount of paperwork. In these Dark Ages, nurses were forbidden to perform such basic tasks, which I thought showed them such disrespect from their own hierarchy. By contrast, doctors were given free rein to teach each other new skills on the job whenever the situation arose, and this kind of ad-hoc learning formed the basis of many a medical career. Hence the old adage 'See One, Do One, Teach One', which applied to everything from taking a blood sample to performing an appendicectomy.

The essential job that really opened up the world to me was my six-month stint in emergency medicine at Bristol Royal Infirmary (BRI), which I had just completed prior to my arrival in Florida. Anything and everything came through that door, and often when you least expected it. The BRI was located at the very heart of Bristol city centre, so there was no such thing as a quiet shift. (It is well known in emergency departments around the world that mentioning the 'Q-word' is considered illegal.) I really enjoyed the unpredictable nature of the work and revelled in the mindset of always expecting the unexpected. Even if the Spanish Inquisition had turned up, we would not have been taken by surprise.

At that time in the UK, emergency medicine was not yet a recognised specialty in its own right, so we had no senior colleagues on hand in the department to guide us. So, the onus fell upon us inexperienced senior house officers to just get the hell on with it. That was, of course, stressful, but also integral to the way of learning in the NHS, which often resembled driving a Formula One car blindfolded around an unfamiliar track; sometimes you just had to put your foot down and hope for the best.

One particular case exemplified this *seat-of-your-pants* learning experience. A forty-three-year-old man was brought in by ambulance, having overdosed on a tricyclic antidepressant, which can be very toxic to the heart. So, it came as no surprise when the patient went into cardiac arrest soon after arriving in the department.

'Ah, shit, he's arrested. Better call the medics.'

'Yep, nurses are onto it. What's the rhythm?'

'Looks like VF [ventricular fibrillation]. He needs a shock.'

Within seconds, we delivered a shock using the defibrillator, which reverted the rhythm back to normal. But this only lasted a minute or so before more bizarre squiggles appeared on the monitor.

'What the hell's that?'

'That's weird. Doesn't look like VF this time.'

The cardiac monitor showed a fast and irregular rhythm that appeared to undulate and twist around the baseline in a sinusoidal fashion. It looked like someone was trying to tune the radio.

'Hey, maybe it's Torsades de Pointes? Does he have a pulse?'

'Nope.'

'Have you seen Torsades before?'

'Nope.'

'Neither have I. Only in a textbook. What shall we do?'

'Dunno. Might as well shock him; he's still in arrest.'

'Hmm…yeah, okay. Can't think of anything else.'

Eight shocks and seven partial recoveries later, the patient finally stabilised. The next day, we heard that he discharged himself from the Intensive Care Unit and walked out.

Mr D and the Cocaine Shooter

Once I had finally finished laughing over the absurdity of Mr D, it was back to bed to sleep off the monster hangover that inevitably followed a night out in Nassau. After weeks of careful research, it became apparent that the severity and duration of these hangovers from hell were directly attributable to one main factor—the discovery of the cocaine shooter.

This lethal cocktail was found loitering on the menu at Piccadilly's, an outdoor bar and restaurant in the centre of Nassau where the evening would kick off at seven o'clock, just as the sun set. Before dinner, it would be fairly quiet, and the friendly bartender, Dave, would guide us through the cocktail menu or try out his latest concoction on us. He was a young, tall, muscular black Bahamian with a dazzling selection of Hawaiian shirts, which were matched only by the brilliance of his gleaming white teeth reflecting the low evening sun. Dirk and I would entertain him by trying to invent our own cocktails while trying not to fall off our barstools. The 'Doctor Death' even made it onto the house menu.

As for the cocaine shooter, it changed the face of drinking as we knew it. The concept of going down the local for a couple of quiet drinks could now include slipping into a coma half an hour later. I really must learn to read the small print.

Dave's smiling face belied the incipient danger as he skilfully poured three perfect layers into a tall wine glass. Sambuca, then Baileys, topped with a generous shot of killer 151-proof rum, which could strip paint at fifty paces.

He handed over a plastic straw and slowly pulled a cigarette lighter from his shirt pocket, pausing for effect, as though about to ask the condemned man for his last request. Once the cocktail was set alight, it was important to empty the glass quickly before the flame melted the straw and the fumes melted your brain. A few minutes later, after recovering one's breath, a warm glow filled the insides and quickly rose to the head, swimming around awhile before massaging the brain with a sensuous buzz. The effect seemed to be contagious, as others around the bar asked to sample the heady mix.

Cocaine Shooters and the odd minor indiscretion aside, a month of relative sobriety seemed to have paid off when I received a fax from Carnival's medical department in Miami. Dr Moises Herszenhorn informed me that I was to be transferred to the ms *Lucky Star* in two days' time. This would be a move to the big-time: a much larger and newer ship, which meant more action, both medically and socially; a more interesting itinerary around the Western Caribbean; and Miami as home port. I saw this as confirmation of Mo's confidence in my ability, which was a boost in itself, and a vindication of my relatively cautious approach. I had been given the stamp of approval by the people who mattered.

And I'd found out Dr Mo's real name!

The fact that my uniform finally arrived on the day I was to transfer ships added to the excitement. For my first month aboard ship, I had had to be content with the few civilian clothes I had brought with me. Although it was initially disappointing and meant that I would not be instantly recognised as the ship's doctor, with all the associated kudos, the plain-clothes look had actually helped my low-profile image.

But now I had gained a month of useful intelligence, Dr Mo's faith, and a healthy tan. I was ready to take that big leap into the limelight and embark on my own voyage of discovery.

4
CAPTAIN'S COCK

The Port of Miami was bustling with activity on a warm Saturday morning. Four major cruise ships were parked along the enormous pier, including the ms *Lucky Star* and, docked immediately behind, its sister ship, the ms *Celebration*. The *Nordic Princess*, the largest cruise ship in the world, and a smaller Caribbean Cruise liner completed the spectacular line-up. Each brilliant white vessel towered above the tarmac, spewing out thousands of sated, sunburned passengers, their mountains of luggage bursting with Caribbean trinkets, T-shirts, and duty-free garbage. Coachloads of fresh faces gathered at the check-in point for the next cruise to paradise, with sun lotion, 'speedos', and stomachs at the ready.

Crew members from all four ships, consisting about forty nationalities, descended upon the nearby crew centre. Here they could buy general provisions, rent hardcore porno videos, or phone their mothers; all three was not unheard of. Inside the crew centre was a large message board that enabled communications between crews from different ships and varying schedules, although this usually amounted to the public display of embarrassing photos or the relaying of urgent messages such as *'Kevin, you're a twat'*.

It was reassuring to see a friendly face amongst all this chaos, and Pete was looking remarkably well. He had been the doctor on the *Celebration* for over six months and was obviously enjoying himself. In contrast to Guy's largely nocturnal existence, Pete had learned to scuba dive, tried some big-game fishing, and been generally more active in his time here. He was looking slim and healthy, which, combined with his six-foot frame and boyish good looks, made him the ideal ship doctor icon. His friendly laid-back nature and excellent doctoring skills added to his appeal, and it was obvious that he had been a big hit on the *Celebration* and could do no wrong in the eyes of Dr Mo. This rather clean-cut image would seem at odds with his alter-ego, Lawsy, but Pete managed to take on the roles of swashbuckling hero and party animal with equal panache. A typical night out could easily involve a bottle of rum (and making an international call from Sheffield to a Mr Ron Bacardi, Nassau, Bahamas, to ask for a refill), a fully clothed dive into the nearest harbour, a few hours in jail, and a sore, bleeding head. All the while maintaining a semblance of poise and a big winning smile. Now then …

Pete took me aboard the *Lucky Star* to meet a few people and show me around. The contrast with the *Carnivale* was striking. Gone was the atmosphere of a patched-up old tug reluctantly ploughing its way through a sea of treacle for its zillionth voyage. The *Lucky Star* was big, bright, and bold, exuding energy and life as it prepared for its next voyage.

Tied up to the pier, it even seemed to champ at the bit in its eagerness to set sail.

Pete only had a short time, so he took me directly to the infirmary to meet the nurses. The space was palatial, with a large main reception area, an adjoining waiting room, and my office, which could be accessed from both. Also, off the main area was a four-bedded ward, a suitably equipped operating room, and a small utility/storage facility.

The plumes of smoke billowing from my office could only mean one of two things. Either my new desk had decided to spontaneously combust, or the inimitable Dr Mo was trying to break the world record for the longest fag-ash while still attached to cigarette during repetitive monologue (current record: 2.05 inches, Dr Mo, Miami, Florida on 15th June 1991).

Through the haze, I could just about make out the intact desk, so it came as no surprise when Mo's gravity-defying quiff floated towards us.

'Paolo! Good to see you!'

Mo beckoned us both into the office, leant back in the chair, and took a deep drag on his cigarette. He was about to launch into one of his carefully crafted yet seemingly impromptu pep talks.

'Close the door behind you, Pete.'

Mo clasped his hands together and leant forward across the desk.

'Now, Paolo, I have heard great reports from the *Carnivale*; you have done very well there,' Mo declared with great enthusiasm. 'But now you should not get big-headed.

This is an opportunity here to really show your skills—it may not be easy, but if you can do what Pete has done on the *Celebration*, they will *love* you here.'

He stood up, turning towards Pete with arms outstretched.

'Look at Pete; he has done tremendous things! They all *love* him!'

Pete smiled and rolled his eyes; this was obviously an old record being played.

Mo continued, 'I am sending over a nurse from the *Celebration* called Linda. I want you to see how she gets on with the others. But now I must go over to the *Celebration* with Pete, so I'll see you next week.'

And with that, Mo departed.

With the ship docked in Miami for only half a day each week, Saturday mornings were to become characterised by these irregular flying visits of our charismatic boss. Whether there had been an incident that week, some in-fighting amongst the nurses, or just some potentially harmful gossip around, Mo always did his homework and visited the captain, security chief, and others before swooping into the infirmary in dramatic cloak-and-dagger fashion. And he would always know absolutely everything that went on. There was certainly no hiding anything from him, and I soon learned that trying to bluff my way out of a tight corner would be the worst possible approach. He could spot a bluff like an expert poker player, or, in the words of former world poker champion Amarillo Slim, 'he could smell a gnat's keester at thirty paces'. I decided to be always completely honest with Mo, and this strategy would prove itself the correct one, with Mo defending my corner and saving my skin time and again over the next year. Still, I never bluff with anything less than four aces.

The three nurses introduced themselves. All were of similar age, about late twenties, and all blonde, but with quite contrasting personalities. Kathy was from Arizona, with a matching fiery temperament, as I was later to find out. Although all smiley and pleasant when required, she had the potential to explode volcanically and become an ultra-bitch from hell. Barbie looked just like her cute namesake doll—petite figure, big blue eyes, and long, flowing blond locks. The effect was uncannily enhanced by her Kentucky drawl and dizzy behaviour, guided by a daily emotional roller-coaster the peaks and troughs of which followed the fate of her latest love interest or broken fingernail. She seemed like the kind of person you didn't want around in a crisis. But she had worked in an emergency room, so obviously she knew everything and didn't mind telling me so.

I heard there had been problems with one of the nurses on the *Celebration*, and I guessed this was why Linda had been transferred here. An Aussie, tall and sturdy with a remarkably psychotic look about her eyes, she did command a rather domineering presence. Mind you, Pete had got on well with her, and she was *almost* British, so maybe she deserved some leeway.

These three diverse characters seemed to me the perfect ingredients for a disaster movie plot, or perhaps a murder mystery.

Death On The Mississippi

Enter legendary murder-mystery-case-solving dwarf detective, Inspector Miniscule Poirot.

Poirrot: 'A most fascinating case. 'Ere we 'ave a brilliant docteur, young and 'andsome wiz a fantastique future as a pioneering brain surgeon. Why, zen, why?

Why does 'ee decide to end it all and take his own life?

Zis is not a case of suicide; zis is murdeur! Murdeur most foul, I say!'

Kathy: 'You mean …?'

Poirrot: 'Yes.'

Linda: 'You mean some charley went and rogered him, ay?'

Barbie: 'Oh Lordy, Lordy! But whaah do ya think it ain't suicaaahde, Mister Per-roh?'

Poirrot: 'Zat was easy. 'Ee was stabbed seventeen times—in ze back! And I 'ef raison to believe zat ze murdereur eez in zis very room!'

(All gasp!)

Kathy: 'Just you hang on one goddamned minute there, mister fucking Parrot, or whatever the hell your name is. You can't just come breezing into *my* infirmary accusing us innocent girls of killing that bastard of a doctor!'

Linda: 'Yeah, you fudge-packing French fairy! He was a right bloody fruitcake that one, ay, deserved a good bashing.'

Barbie: 'Oh my Good Lord! This is all too much for li'l old me! Ah think ah'm gonna faint now in this sultry, sultry heat. See y'all!'

(Faints dramatically to floor while maintaining perfect hairstyle.)

Curtain falls

The *Lucky Star* glided serenely out of the Port of Miami, following Biscayne Boulevard and its multi-million-dollar homes dotted along the waterfront, and into Miami Sound. Soon we would be sailing in open sea and setting a path around the eastern tip of Cuba and on to Cozumel, Mexico.

I took a moment to pause and take in the scene from the top deck, overlooking the aft lido deck where the party was already under way. With glorious clear blue sky from horizon to horizon, the warm afternoon sun at my back, and perfectly caressing breeze at my skin, I felt fantastic. I listened to the gentle swish of the bow cutting an effortless path through the shimmering glass sea—but only until the calypso band cranked up the fifty-third rendition of 'Feelin' Hot! Hot! Hot!'

My attention turned to the deck party, and I felt a stirring in my loins. I could hardly believe my eyes; fifty scantily clad college girls frolicking around and getting drunk on sparkling wine, looking forward to a week of fun. *Well, ladies,* I thought, *you've come to the right place.*

'Ah, doctor!' bellowed the captain across the deck as he approached with his entourage. He was very young compared to Fornari and had the typical appearance of a southern Italian: thick, dark, curly hair, a short stature, and an old-fashioned moustache.

'Welcome to the Lucky Star! Don't forget my party at six o'clock, okay?'

'Of course, I'll see you there,' I managed to reply as he swept past me and down to the lido deck with his henchmen. No doubt there were some urgent navigational calculations to attend to at the deck party.

So, he was having a party? That long tradition on Carnival Cruises to have a formal dress night where everybody puts on their sequins and dickie bows and enjoys more cheap sparkling wine and suspicious canapes, hosted by the main man. The Captain's Cocktail Party would be the perfect way to kick things off.

Captain Mario Gambino seemed like a friendly chap, and the fact that he was only thirty-six years old, and Sicilian suggested to me that we had a few things in common and might get along well.

It was Linda's first night onboard too, so we decided to stick together for a while. I could soon see why Pete had got on well with her, because she had a great sense of humour and a razor-sharp way with words. Linda complained that the other nurses on the *Celebration* had been bitches and had stirred up trouble behind her back. I didn't really care what had gone on before, as long as my nurses didn't cause trouble here.

I prepared myself for the party, putting on my brand-new formal uniform. With black shoes and dress trousers, plain white dress shirt, and standard-issue black bowtie, the uniform at first seemed fairly dull. But the crowning glory was the short, waist-length white jacket, complete with gold buttons and topped by the black epaulettes across the shoulders. These epaulettes bore the three golden stripes that indicated senior officer status, plus the red and gold caduceus, the ancient Greek depiction of two serpents winding their way around a golden staff topped by wings, which is often used to symbolise medicine in the USA. This transformed the ensemble into a radiant beacon of power.

Or maybe I now looked like a cross between Sid James's *Carry On Up the Khyber* and *Fawlty Towers*' hapless waiter, Manuel!

The Captain's Cocktail Party on the *Carnivale* had been a rather dull affair, as the weary Captain Fornari saw it as a tiresome chore. He detested the passengers and was loath to appear in public, let alone entertain the masses. The veteran master reeled off the same old 'Welcome aboard' message each week in a flat monotone. The only interest remaining was whether he could beat the previous weeks' time before disappearing.

Gambino, however, was still basking in the glory of being recently appointed as captain, and with his youth and natural vitality bursting from every seam, he strutted around the ship as though he owned it. He may as well have, as he bustled around fiddling, adjusting, and making things just how *he* wanted. I could see how he had made his way up the ladder to be captain—he was smart, looked sharp and decisive, and overflowed with energy and confidence. It was also plain to see that these attributes drove an enormous ego, and he loved to be the centre of attention.

The party kicked off with a long line-up of new passengers in their most gaudy outfits, eager to meet the ship's captain and shake his hand before entering the gala lounge. Captain Fornari had considered passengers as harbouring all sorts of unhygienic and potentially fatal diseases, and he would avoid physical contact at all costs. Gambino, on the other hand, was direct from the Hollywood school of public relations. Always nothing less than charming, he welcomed the fawning guests having their picture taken with him, with big, beaming smiles all round. But it was when the young ladies came into view, all coiffed and perfumed, that the glint appeared in his eye. It was abundantly clear that my new master's charisma and powerful position made him a hit with the starry-eyed ladies.

Once inside the gala lounge, the champagne and cocktails began to flow, and the thousand new passengers packed into this amazing three-storey-high theatre eagerly anticipating the evening's entertainment. I was sipping my champagne a bit nervously because after the captain's welcoming speech, all ten senior officers were to be introduced on stage. If the *Carnivale* was anything to go by, it would all be over in a very dull five minutes, but there was something about this ship and Captain Gambino that told me otherwise.

Then the lights dimmed, and the crowd hushed. A single spotlight soared up to the roof, sixty feet above the stage, as the orchestra launched into the opening bars of the *Rocky* theme tune, 'Eye of the Tiger'.

And there was the master, sixty feet up in the air inside a steel cage, tightly grabbing hold of the metal bars and grinning from ear to ear. The crowd went wild with delight, and the crew wet their pants with laughter. The bright spot then followed the beaming Gambino as his cage slowly descended to the continued beat of the *Rocky* anthem. Once landed, he leapt from the steel cube, hamming it up nicely, to be received by his adoring audience. He was loving every second of it, and he milked the rapturous applause like a true pro. He obviously loved himself tremendously, I thought.

But fair play to him; he knew how to play the game, and the passengers loved it.

Once the audience had settled down after Gambino's extraordinary entrance, it was time to get back to the script. He grabbed the microphone and began the introductions.

'As captain of this vessel, it is my great pleasure and privilege to wish you all a warm welcome aboard the beautiful ms *Lucky Star!*'

Gambino employed his well-honed skills of timing and delivery, pausing to acknowledge the crowd's warm response.

'And now I am pleased to present the ship's senior officers. The staff captain, Giuseppe Messina!'

Up stepped his right-hand man to ripples of applause. The laid-back Messina sauntered across the stage to take his place next to his master. Stocky and dark-skinned with a luxuriously virile head of hair, the bearded one soon unleashed his most steamy look upon the crowd. The ladies in the house responded to his big brown eyes and seductive smile with a burst of excited applause and lurid catcalls. He and Gambino feigned surprise and boyish innocence at this response, but both could be seen licking their lips with excited anticipation of the forthcoming seven days at sea.

Not having met the other officers yet, I took this opportunity to form a quick picture of them all in my head, noting any who I may have to be wary of as each went up in turn.

Next up was the chief engineer, a balding little Italian with gold teeth who was knocking back the champagne with boyish glee.

Verdict: No problem.

Radio Officer Santos: fifty-five, fat, with a face like a bucket of smashed crabs.

Verdict: No problem.

Interesting to note, however, that the ship's radio officer was Venezuelan, and despite allegedly speaking fluent English, it was impossible to understand a single word he spoke:

Santos: 'Mayday! Mayday! Mayday! ms *Lucky Star* has hit an iceberg and is sinking.'

Junior Coastguard: 'Sir! Sir! I have a message coming through on the emergency frequency. Blah blah blah, mucky car—shit a burger, and it's stinking!'

Senior Coastguard: 'That'll be those pesky college kids again. Just ignore it.'

Then the hotel manager, David Gardner: short, smarmy looking, with a limp moustache.

Verdict: Danger, treat with caution.

The chief purser, Neil Davis: tall and gangly with glasses. Seemed a bit wimpy.

Verdict: Nerd, no problem.

Captain Gambino continued with his introductions.

'And now we have the ship's physician, Doctor Paolo Amodeo!'

Up the steps I went, wondering what kind of reception I would get. I made my way across the brightly lit stage to take up my position in the senior officer line-up, and I couldn't help but grin from ear to ear as the applause rang out and cameras flashed. Much to everyone's amusement, some women at the front began to feign illness, crying out, 'I'm sick! I'm sick! I need to see the doctor!'

'He looks so young!' was the chorus from the floor. Although no room keys were thrown (which had happened to Pete), it was clear that this moment marked the threshold of a new era in the exploits of the young medic. However, the warm reception didn't go unnoticed by Gambino. Eyebrows were raised, and he and Messina made light of it with the crowd, but I could sense the undercurrent in their long Sicilian stares at me across the stage.

The battle lines had been drawn, and the gloves were off.

Immediately after the cocktail party, I was invited to dine at the captain's table, which was encouraging. Until I realised that my first official duty as senior officer was to act as cannon-fodder. I took up my seat according to the named positions at the large round table and soon found that my job was to entertain the Dweedlebaums while Gambino and Messina worked on the girls over their side of the playing field. But throughout the length of the four-course dinner, I couldn't help but notice that the captain's rather attractive young consort seemed to pay him scant attention and kept looking over towards me. I tried to avoid encouraging her, but Gambino's chagrin was noticeable by the end of the meal. But with Mo's words reverberating in my head, I sloped off quietly and left them to it.

I caught up with Linda, and we wandered around the main deck, getting our bearings and checking out the bars.

'Hey, Linda, that Captain's Cocktail Party was unbelievable!'

I was still bemused by the whole event.

'Yeah, it was a right hoot, ay!' Linda replied, giggling.

'Compared to the *Carnivale*, it was like being on another planet. I've never seen anything like it!'

'Well, maybe that's why over here they call it the Captain's Cock!'

'Ha! Yes … of course, how bloody appropriate,' I concluded, the indelible image of Gambino's macho grand entrance still fresh in my mind.

Walking up the main drag, we heard shouts and giggles from behind.

'There he is, there he is!'

I was then accosted by a gaggle of six tipsy, middle-aged groupies who had apparently been seeking me out since the cocktail party. They were all nurses from New Jersey and wanted a photograph with the ship`s doctor, so I duly obliged. Stardom at last!

After a few more photo stops, I inevitably found my way into the disco. It was packed with all sorts of people: marauding gangs of college girls hitting the cocktails; some sober honeymooners wishing they'd gone to Barbados instead; awkward, gangly adolescents sporting the latest teenage uniform of baseball cap turned backwards, McDonald's acne (with cheese), and ridiculously baggy shorts; and the anxious parents trying to keep track of their potentially wayward sixteen-year-old daughter. Add the ubiquitous Italian officers cruising the dark perimeter of this arena, and you had the recipe for some fireworks.

I introduced myself to a group of officers who looked like they were having fun. A couple of American pursers, the Jamaican chief steward, the English casino manager, and Robert, a young English assistant F&B manager. All were grouped around the chief engineer, who held their attention with his latest dirty joke.

'Now let's Spoof for the next round of drinks!' suggested the chief, grinning mischievously.

Everyone agreed, and I was given a crash course in Spoof: three coins each, any number of which, including zero, to be placed secretly in your right hand. The person who guesses the total number of coins in all hands wins the round and drops out. The last person remaining loses the game and buys all the drinks. It looked easy at first, with luck appearing to be the major factor, but after a few rounds, it became apparent that a great deal of bluff and counter bluff was involved, especially when few players remain. How many coins did my opponent choose last time? What will they do this time? Why did he call three? Does he have two and put me on one, or is his hand empty, figuring mine full?

With eight or more thirsty players, all familiar with the most extravagant cocktails this side of Mars, a bad call could prove expensive. Before I knew it, the game had reached its climax, and I found myself up against the wily old chief engineer. The final head-to-head showdown worked on a best-of-three basis, a test of nerve and guile.

A bit of psychological analysis would be in order here, I thought. Searching my memory banks for inspiration, I recalled a gem of basic poker strategy. In Herbert O Yardley's autobiographical classic, *The Education of a Poker Player*, the young Yardley is given advice on good poker play by his mentor, James Montgomery. Monty illustrates one of the basic psychological ploys by quoting an excerpt from Edgar Allan Poe's *The Purloined Letter*, which concludes that the tactics you employ should depend on an assessment of your opponent's intellect—is he a simpleton, or a step or two above that?

I sized up the chief. He was surely no simpleton and knew the game well. But he had lost all the previous rounds. So, was he smart and unlucky, or …?

Inevitably, all this academic pondering proved too much for my simpleton brain, and I lost 2-0.

'Okay, so it's one Long Island iced tea, two rum runners, a strawberry daiquiri, one frozen margarita with no salt, two Alabama slammers, and one screaming orgasm!'

Hell, this was a long way from Sheffield, where ordering a rum and coke in the wrong bar could incur a hostile reception from some of the hard-nosed locals.

'Not having a pint, lad? Bloody poof!'

'What kind of poncey drink do ya call that? Nowt wrong with Tetley's!'

A gentle tap on the shoulder rescued me from the warm-beer-and-Yorkshire-pudding flashback.

'Hey, Doc!'

Before me stood the captain's dinner guest. Minus the captain. I tried to remain somewhat distant and formal in case El Capitano was watching.

'Hello, nice to meet you again,' I replied stoically. But I found it impossible to ignore those dazzling blue eyes, complimented by her figure-hugging sequinned dress.

'Ahem, where's the captain? I thought you were his "special guest"?'

'I dumped him. Couldn't keep his hands off me, the creep!' she replied, grimacing.

Interesting news, I thought.

'Oh. Really? That's a shame. Why don't we go and get a drink?' I suggested, still trying to maintain an air of polite sophistication.

'Great. I'll have a sex on the beach!'

All thoughts of pseudo-sophistication went straight out the window. The innuendo was obvious, and the lights had instantly changed from a cautionary amber to green for go!

Now I had to make a difficult decision. Do I heed Mo's warning, play The Game, and politely keep my distance, so avoiding incurring the wrath of the master?

Or do I go for it and test out the infirmary operating table?

No contest for a budding surgeon.

5

ILLEGAL ALIENS AND THE BALLS OF FIRE

Springtime in the Caribbean was the best of seasons—warm, sunny weather and mostly calm seas, free from the threat of hurricanes that brewed over the summer months. The scene was now set for enjoying the cruise-ship lifestyle and getting to know the people I would be living and working with for the foreseeable future.

Linda had quickly become my best friend onboard, as we shared that British-type dry sense of humour that some Americans just didn't get. As for Barbie and Kathy, we never quite hit it off like I had with the Aussie, but we often shared a few drinks and some good laughs in the crew bar after work. Besides, Kathy had teamed up with Krishna, the tall and handsome Indian F&B manager, so we didn't really see much of her outside of work hours as their spicy romance blossomed.

My new job on the *Lucky Star* was, as expected, busier than the *Carnivale*. But we rarely encountered serious medical cases, mainly due to the relatively young age of *Carnival*'s passengers. This contrasted with what one might expect on a months-long voyage with a more traditional, elderly cruise crowd.

Morning clinics were mostly made up of patients looking for hangover cures, treatment for seasickness, or replacement medication for forgotten tablets. Add to that the usual coughs and colds and some minor injuries, and that just about summed up the workload. Occasionally, we had a genuinely ill patient, but by and large we had to find our intellectual challenges elsewhere.

New crew members to the ship were expected to undergo a routine medical examination in their first week aboard, and this was very boring kind of work. So, after a while, Linda and I decided to have a little fun with it and invented a fake One-Minute Medical:

Before the new recruit entered the examination room, a fresh ten-dollar bill was placed on the floor.

If they spotted the note easily, that would complete the visual assessment: *Check*.

When they bent over to pick up the ten-dollar bill, that would confirm spinal integrity: *Check*.

While leaning forward, next came a surprise digital rectal examination to assess the prostate and lower gastrointestinal tract: *Check. Check.*

The resulting loud exclamation confirmed a functional respiratory system: *Check*.

If a punch was then thrown in my direction, this showed an intact nervous system: *Check*.

Getting used to dealing with American patients was one of the trickier tasks. They were certainly more demanding than British patients, who were used to the free service of the NHS, and as such were less likely to complain. A British passenger who sprained their ankle would apologise and berate themselves while hobbling to the infirmary for help.

'Silly old me! I missed the step and twisted my ankle. Sorry to waste your time.'

In stark contrast, I encountered several Americans, especially New Yorkers, who preferred to make a mountain out of a molehill and displayed a far more litigious attitude.

'Where's the goddamned sign saying *Mind your step*?' they would shout on entering the infirmary by wheelchair. 'I'm gonna sue the ass off this company! Get me some ice and an ACE bandage, now!'

Pete also recounted a case that had taken this American tendency to seek legal recourse to an unbelievably extreme level. Onboard the *Celebration* while at sea, Pete had revived a passenger who had gone into cardiac arrest, and he managed to save his life. The ungrateful patient had made such an amazingly good recovery thanks to Pete and his team that towards the end of the cruise, he called his lawyer and attempted to sue Pete for giving atropine before adrenaline (epinephrine in US), in contravention of the American Heart Association guidelines at the time. Fortunately, the case was taken no further, but it highlighted the disrespectful nature and money-grabbing attitude of some of our patients.

It also took a while for me to get used to charging patients for their medical care. An American doctor who I saw as a patient became very irate when we gave him the bill from the ship's Sail & Sign system. He declared he should be subject to something called 'professional courtesy', claiming that he shouldn't be charged a cent. Never having worked in private practice before, I had no idea what he was talking about.

Nevertheless, each patient was treated appropriately, and I quickly learned that part of the job was exercising good public relations in addition to medical management.

Public relations were one thing. Behind the scenes was another.

Most evenings would invariably be spent cruising along the main promenade deck, socialising, drinking, and talent-spotting. Linda and I were keen to make some new friends onboard, and Rob, the English F&B guy, always seemed to pop up somewhere near the disco with a friendly smile on his face.

Pleased to see Rob, I put my hand on his shoulder. 'Hi, Rob, what's happening?'

'Oh, the usual. I've just lost at Spoof, so I'm off to the bar,' replied the diminutive Rob as he used the corner of his jacket to wipe the steam off his glasses.

Linda commiserated, 'Bad luck again, ay. Hey, Rob, have you seen Giovanni around?'

'I think he's over on the other side of the bar, coning,' Rob smirked.

'What?' I was momentarily stunned.

In the medical world, the term 'coning' indicates a dire emergency. It describes the pre-terminal situation of someone who has severely raised intracranial pressure (within their skull). This can cause the brainstem to get squashed down into the foramen magnum, the hole at the base of the skull, forming a cone-shaped deformity of this vital part of the brain, a prelude to incipient death. A vision of the 'coning' Giovanni appeared before me: the poor young electrician becoming rapidly unconscious and collapsing on the dancefloor, his eyes rolling around in their sockets, and his body undergoing violent spasms while everyone else continued to perform the 'Electric Slide' in perfect formation around him.

It took me a few seconds to pull myself together as my brain processed the information.

'Giovanni is doing what?' I asked incredulously.

'Ha-ha,' Linda laughed. 'I know what you're thinking. That's hilarious!'

'So, what is…coning?'

Linda took a moment to gather herself from her fit of laughter.

'We call the passengers "Cones", but obviously we don't let them know that. It's from the TV show *Saturday Night Live*. You know, the one with Dan Ackroyd, who made up The Coneheads.'

'I've no idea. What's a Conehead?'

'Well, The Coneheads are a bunch of aliens living on earth, ay, and they are known for their stupidity and massive appetites for food and beer—hence the Cones!'

'Ah, I see. That's brilliant. And "coning" is …?'

'Yeah, so "coning" is trying to get off with a passenger, ay.'

Fraternising with passengers was technically not permitted aboard ship. The higher your rank, the more you could get away with, but it still paid to be discreet. Merely talking to someone in the bar would attract attention, and any suggestive behaviour or public display of affection could mean serious trouble. Dancing was allowed but avoided at all costs, as all eyes would be watching your every move. This resulted in 'The Officers' Shuffle'—the stiff, plodding, nervous gait adopted by most officers when asked by a passenger to dance with them. It would be impolite to refuse, but most officers would try to find an excuse not to dance and avoid being put under the spotlight. Quite often, the invitation would come from an older woman, and this was fine; she would have the pleasure of dancing with a ship's officer, and we had the opportunity to check out the girls on the dance floor while remaining under the radar.

Once the evening's target had been spotted, it wouldn't take much to get things going, and quite often it would be the passenger who would make the first move. I soon learned that American girls were not backwards in coming forward. A bit of eye contact here, some musical chairs there, and before you knew it, they would be whisked away for a guided tour of the ship. Sometimes it would be a romantic walk out on deck under the stars, or a few more drinks at one of the shows. If the passion was searingly obvious from the outset, then an immediate rendezvous down at the infirmary would be arranged, followed by a quick decision between the operating table or my quarters.

The only place strictly off limits was a passenger's cabin. If things went wrong and they made a complaint, then you would be leaving yourself extremely exposed if it all took place in her room. If you were going to dabble, it was much safer done on your own turf. Even then, you would have to run the gauntlet not to get rumbled. Evading the eyes of Gambino's mob in the disco was relatively easy, but the next morning would provide them with another opportunity to catch me out. My cabin was situated just a few doors away from the officers' mess, and come breakfast time, The Game recommenced. Any passenger walking past the mess could be spotted instantly and would have come from only two other rooms. So, if the young lady stayed the night, she would have to do a pre-breakfast escape or run like hell past the mess.

All these cloak-and-dagger antics added that extra bit of intrigue, and the girls didn't mind—it just added to the fun!

After a couple of cocktails in the disco, we decided to move on. It was clear that Linda fancied that young Italian electrician, Giovanni, and didn't really wish to observe his coning exploits at firsthand. So, she headed back to her cabin to take out her frustration; Linda had become rather obsessed with her latest fitness video purchase, *Buns of Steel*.

Aside from the pulsating disco, there was plenty of other entertainment on offer. The main auditorium staged nightly shows, ranging from musical theatre and dance performances to magicians and comedy acts. Other venues hosted a rock band, a piano bar, and of course the bingo.

There were also some 'fly-in' acts who would join the ship for just a few days at a time, and some of these were quite memorable characters who would join the resident staff and officers in the ship's crew bar for a few drinks after their show.

The comedian Gene Merola was great fun, and his late-night act was side-splittingly good, and close to the bone. I even remember one of his best jokes:

> Marriage is a strange thing. When you first get together, it's real passionate, and bam! You're banging each other whenever you can. After a while, it calms down a bit, and sex becomes maybe a daily event. Then a few years down the track, things start to get a bit boring, and it's maybe once a week, then perhaps once a month. Eventually, after ten years, it's just oral sex: you pass each other in the hallway and it's 'Fuck you!' 'No, fuck *you*!'

Thursdays offered a chance to get off the ship and take a break in Ocho Rios on Jamaica's north coast. I was struck by how the islands of the Caribbean offered such amazing diversity. Grand Cayman Island, which the *Lucky Star* visited for half a day each Wednesday, was very small and flat, with picture-postcard beaches and a burgeoning economy based on offshore banking. Many passengers would take an afternoon excursion to swim with and feed the stingrays on a sandbar just off Seven Mile Beach. As for me, I was technically not allowed off the ship, as the *Lucky Star* did not dock into a port but simply weighed anchor a mile or so offshore. From here, the passengers would be ferried ashore by a series of small vessels known as tenders.

By contrast, Jamaica was the third-largest island in the Caribbean and mostly covered by lush, mountainous rainforests harvesting many fruits and spices, and it was famous for its Blue Mountain brand of coffee beans. Its capital, Kingston, was notorious for its very high crime rate and gang violence, and poverty was widespread on the island. But Jamaica did nourish a rich cultural heritage, being home to reggae legend Bob Marley and a getaway destination for Ian Fleming, who famously owned a villa called Goldeneye near Ocho Rios, where he wrote all of his James Bond novels in the 1950s and 60s.

Ocho Rios itself was really nothing more than a sleepy fishing village, and most passengers would spend the day clambering up Dunn's River Falls or tubing down the White River, can of Red Stripe beer in hand. The ship's crew would try to find alternative activities, and I would often visit the local Chinese restaurant for lunch, then go for a walk around the village with Linda, taking photos of the local fruit markets and the colourful backstreet life.

But some of the alternative activities sought out by some of the crew turned out to have less-than-desirable consequences.

One Thursday afternoon, the guitarist from the ship's rock band was seen walking back through Jamaican customs near the pier with a basketball in hand. For some reason, this aroused the suspicion of one of the customs officers, who asked the musician to bounce the ball—it dropped to the floor and stayed put, not bouncing an inch. It turned out the basketball was heavily packed with marijuana, and so the guilty muso never made it back onto the ship with his red-hot ball.

Crew clinic on Friday afternoons regularly included a gaggle of deckhands, galley workers, and cabin stewards who had made the most of a precious half day off by visiting the local Ocho Rios whorehouse. So, every week, it was essentially the Friday Clap Clinic. Presentations ranged from a standard sore knob or funny rash to the more extreme complaint that their balls were on fire!

Every Thursday another 'fly-in' entertainer, Manuel Zuniga, would board the *Lucky Star* at Ocho Rios, just before we set off on our thirty-six-hour return leg to Miami. This voyage happened to cross the path of some fast-moving currents, which later coalesced as the Gulf Stream along the US east coast and across the North Atlantic. So, the *Lucky Star* rocked and rolled through choppy seas every Thursday night—not exactly ideal conditions for a juggling act!

The enthralled audience would hold their breath watching Zuniga steady himself on stage, the ship lurching from side to side as he went through his act of increasingly difficult routines. But Manuel was one of the world's best and would only rarely make a mistake, perhaps once every few weeks when the seas were particularly rough. As his show reached its climax, we could barely watch. Manuel would gather himself for a moment, throw several billiard balls about thirty feet in the air, and, in a heart-stopping blaze of glory, catch each rock-hard ball in his mouth one by one.

I sure didn't fancy being his dentist.

My main concern was that if the ship suddenly listed at the wrong moment, he might get a billiard ball square in the forehead. But his juggling brilliance always shone through, and thankfully he survived unscathed each time, to the relief and appreciation of the entire crowd. I was especially grateful that we didn't have to deal with a *real* case of coning. The champion juggler would take his bow and then head to the crew bar, where he took on all comers in our weekly darts tournament. Inevitably, he always came out on top, and usually beat me into second place.

Every six months the US Coastguard came onboard in Miami to inspect the ship and survey the safety procedures. The company would be given only a few days' notice to ready the crew. I had been involved in several practice runs already, and the role of the medical team was straightforward: answer the emergency call, locate the casualty, treat appropriately at the scene, then stretcher them to the infirmary.

The alarm sounded—three short blasts of the ship's whistle, indicating the commencement of the drill. Linda, Barbie, and I donned our lifejackets and gas masks and waited for the emergency call. Linda answered when it came,

'They want us to go to the aft dining room; it's a fire,' she told us.

'How many casualties?' I asked.

'Three.'

'Okay. Linda, you come with me. Bring the defibrillator. I'll take the emergency bag and the radio. Barbie, you stay here and hold the fort. I'll keep in touch by radio.'

'But the stretcher team haven't arrived yet!' Barbie reminded me.

A few minutes later, our assigned stretcher crew pitched up. And what a motley crew. The crack emergency stretcher team comprised three Korean laundry boys with less muscle between them than a Kentucky Fried Chicken wing, a sixty-five-year-old Haitian cabin steward with emphysema, and two Guatemalan busboys kitted out in shorts and flip-flops. Something told me that these boys had been hand-picked.

As we made our way down to the scene of the fire, I listened in to Emergency Channel 1A on the hand-held VHF radio.

'Starboard fire doors now closed. The aft dining room now sealed off. Over,' announced the fire chief.

'Is the fire contained?' came his master's voice.

'Yes,' replied the Coastguard inspector. *'The fire crew are now hosing the blaze. Over.'*

'How many casualties are there?' enquired Gambino.

'Six. Two with serious burns and four with smoke inhalation. Where is the medical team?'

I spoke into the radio, 'Medical team is on its way. Can you confirm number of casualties? Over.'

'Six,' the inspector repeated.

'Okay. Infirmary, do you copy?'

A moment of silence was followed by some hissing and crackling noises before Barbie replied like an excited child.

Illegal Aliens and the Balls of Fire

'This is the infirmary; I can hear you!' Barbie was almost overwhelmed by the miracle that was modern technology.

I tried to plan ahead.

'Barbie, we have six casualties. Stand by with another stretcher team, but stay here for now. Captain, I need someone to meet us in the aft lobby. Can you send a man to guide us to the casualties?'

'Roger. There'll be someone in the aft lobby to meet you.'

Our team manoeuvred the cumbersome bucket stretcher down the narrow stairwells towards the lobby. The poor old cabin steward was already struggling for breath, and we hadn't even picked up the patient yet, so I helped and gave him a break.

'We have a problem with the pump pressure!' yelled the fire chief.

The chief engineer came into the fray. *'I know, I know! We'll have to change to hydrant twelve, by the kitchen stairwell. Can you do that?'*

'Okay. Hydrant twelve. It'll take a few minutes.'

It sounded like the imaginary fire was getting out of control, I surmised as we clattered into the aft lobby. There to meet us was Captain Gambino himself, all decked out in his peaked sea captain's hat and Ray Ban 'Wayfarer' sunglasses. Damn, that fire must be bright!

'Doctor! This way, this way!' he gestured frantically, pointing towards the heavy doors leading to the dining room before rushing off.

Our team re-grouped, pushed the doors to one side, and piled in with the gusto of an elite commando unit. We were greeted with surprise by several of the fire crew in full firefighting kit, struggling with the hoses in which they had become entangled, which were like giant squid tentacles. I looked around for the casualties but was stopped in my tracks by the Coastguard inspector, wielding his notorious clipboard. He looked somewhat alarmed to see us.

'Who are you?' he enquired.

'I am the doctor,' I stated emphatically.

Wasn't it obvious who we were? I indicated the gang of sweaty men behind me exhibiting various states of exhaustion.

'And this is the stretcher team,' I added.

'Well, that may be so, but you have just entered through that fire door and into this blazing inferno. You are all dead!'

He looked down to his clipboard to make a note: '*Medical team killed by fire.*'

I was furious. Gambino had made me look a fool by directing us straight into the fire. There was no other explanation. He could have ordered anybody to meet the medical team, but no, the captain had made a point of doing it himself and exacting a twisted revenge.

His fire drill move had all the hallmarks of a premeditated vendetta, and I felt like it was now *my* balls that had been set alight.

I would really have to start watching my back.

6

THE GREAT ESCAPE

Despite Gambino's act of calculated subterfuge, life was still good, and there was always fun to be had. May 12th was International Nurses Day, the anniversary of Florence Nightingale's birth. So, I decided to give Linda, Kathy, and Barbie an unofficial day off and made sure I was available in the infirmary to cover for their absence. As I was filling in as nurse for the day, I dressed up accordingly by donning a complete nurse's uniform and a fluffy blonde wig borrowed from the entertainment director.

Fortunately, it wasn't a busy day, so I had time to sit down and write a poem to mark the occasion:

> *Nurses Day comes once a year,*
> *And makes me feel a little queer.*
> *At work all day and with no choice,*
> *With nice white skirt and high-pitched voice.*
>
> *With a dressing-change here, a Sail & Sign there,*
> *Paint my nails and dye my hair (blonde).*
> *The doctor not in? What an abhorrence!*
> *Never mind, just call me Florence.*

Or I could be Linda; I'll help you heal,
With my razor wit and buns of steel.
Or maybe Kathy, big on trauma,
But usually found eating beef korma.

I could be Barbie, but heart don't fail.
During cardiac massage, I could break a nail.
But enough of all this girlie chat,
I'm putting on my doctor's hat.

Nurse! Make the coffee! Nurse! Get an ACE!
Come over here and sit on my face!
That's more like it, that's the way.
Oh, I can't wait for Doctor's Day.

Later that week, life took an unexpected turn. This event put a seething Captain Gambino onto the back foot and had everyone on edge for weeks to come.

Gambino's affair with one of the young English dancers was no secret to most of the crew. She was only in her early twenties but by no means immature or naïve like many of her starry-eyed young colleagues, who saw her as manipulative and untrustworthy. As such, she was not well liked, and her close association with the captain and his cronies made her even more dangerous. Much of her spare time was spent hanging around with this chosen few, and she had been smart enough to learn some Italian. Soon she began referring to the master by his first name, Mario, in general conversation, and she would constantly remind everybody of the fact that they were big buddies, although the true nature of their relationship could never be mentioned directly.

Their romantic liaison had continued for months and bestowed her with such power that it led to much friction at work, with any problems or disagreements among the entertainment staff being relayed directly to the captain himself. It was ideal for him too. Not only were his ego and sexual appetite taken care of by the young Claire, who was fifteen years his junior, but she was also well positioned and shrewd enough to act as his chief spy, and she took on this mantle with relish.

Ship-board affairs were, of course, nothing unusual. The Italian officers spent nine months at sea before taking a three-month break, and with all the attractive young dancers and Scandinavian casino staff at their mercy, it was inevitable that sparks would fly. For some, there was genuine romance, love, and even marriage to be found. But many of the Italians had wives and families back home, and this did not deter their pursuit of ship-board passion. This saddened me at first, but later I realised that it would surely be impossible for anybody to maintain a monogamous relationship when spending so much time apart. They had chosen a life at sea; it was their career, so perhaps their wives understood. So, news of Gambino's affair with Claire, aside from the spy ring, didn't really cause too much of a stir.

At least not until his wife and two young children came onboard for a three-week holiday.

Gambino had the audacity to not only introduce his lovely wife to mistress Claire, but also encouraged the young dancer to act as child-minder to his offspring. Even worse than this, he continued his affair while his unknowing spouse was onboard. This arrogance and total disregard for the mother of his children did not go unnoticed, and many people lost any respect they may have had for him.

One person who took a particular interest in all these goings-on was the new Genovese staff captain, Stefano Baresi. It was well known that he and Gambino hated each other, and it was more than just the usual Genovese-Sicilian tribal feud between two of the great maritime hubs of the north and south of Italy. There was an obvious personality clash. The tall and sturdy Baresi was renowned for his authoritarianism and dour nature, Gambino for his flexibility and flamboyance. But their mutual contempt knew no bounds and strongly suggested some previous major altercation. Baresi was much older too, and he must have resented the fact that he would probably never make it to the rank of captain.

And now he saw his chance to land Gambino in trouble, he wasn't going to let it pass. If he could only find a way to publicly reveal the affair while the master's wife was onboard, Gambino would find himself in dire straits. Not only would his marriage be in jeopardy, but perhaps also his entire credibility and captain's stripes.

Then one Sunday morning, Baresi's golden opportunity presented itself like an answered prayer. The Sabbath was a sea day, a day of rest for many onboard. At ten o'clock sharp every week, the captain would lead a group of senior officers on an inspection tour of the ship, pointing out fixtures in need of repair or areas requiring a polish and suchlike. This Sunday, however, Gambino was missing.

Baresi asked the first officer if he knew of the captain's whereabouts.

'No idea,' came the stony reply, the first officer pulling a long face.

'Well, he must be somewhere. Go and try his quarters; he must be with his wife.'

The first officer reluctantly put down his coffee and slowly wandered over to the master's quarters, just near the main control room on the bridge. He soon returned, and with a slight tilt of the head and inhaling sharply through clenched teeth, reported back.

'Nope, he's not with her.'

By now, the other senior officers had gathered: the hotel manager, David Gardner of the Limp Moustache, the chief steward, F&B manager, chief engineer, and chief purser.

'Let's try his pager,' suggested Neil Davis, sensibly. The first officer again followed orders with some reluctance, picking up the telephone receiver like one would an unexploded bomb, then pressing the keys with all the urgency of a snail on its way to a French restaurant. Five minutes went by with no answer from Gambino. Baresi's agitation was palpable, and the chiefs were becoming concerned. Where could he be? Was he alright? There was only so far you could go on a ship.

That was when the revelation came to Baresi, and he suddenly sensed where the captain was. He must have been with Claire. Even though the affair was common knowledge, to be caught in flagrante delicto would be a huge embarrassment to Gambino, not to mention the likelihood of his wife finding out. But how could he catch him, with witnesses, *and* make it appear accidental, all at the same time?

In a flash, Baresi made a beeline for the microphone of the ship's public address system.

'Captain Gambino, please report to the bridge. I repeat. Captain Gambino, please report to the bridge immediately. Thank you.'

Such a cunning move. This message was heard all around the ship except for the crew quarters below deck. If Gambino was where Baresi thought he was, he would not have heard the message. As expected, Mrs Gambino came running up to the bridge, right on cue.

'What's happening? Is something wrong?' enquired the master's wife anxiously.

Baresi calculated his next move. 'We cannot find your husband. He is not answering his pager, and nobody has seen him.'

'So … what do you mean?' She was getting worried now and had taken the bait perfectly.

Baresi continued, 'I think I know where he might be. I'm sure he's fine. Why don't you wait here, and I'll go with the chiefs and try to find him.'

On hearing this, the previously lethargic first officer sat bolt upright. He then went pale, broke into a sweat, and left the bridge immediately, gesturing to the first mate to follow him out. They had no time to waste if they were to save their boss from public humiliation. The race was on; Baresi trying to usher the chiefs down to the crew quarters as fast as possible while Gambino's henchmen tried to stall them and desperately get word to Gambino that a one-man lynch mob was on its way with a group of VIP spectators in tow.

'Cabin inspection!' bellowed the staff captain, banging loudly on the cabin door. After a few moments, Claire answered with obvious hesitation in her voice.

'Just a moment, I'm not dressed.'

But this excuse only served to fuel the staff's suspicions. I listened carefully to the furtive noises emanating from Claire's cabin. Was she alone? Was the master really in there?

'Open up; this is the staff captain!' He was getting impatient now, his face reddening. The junior officers shuffled around, muttering expletives and checking the corridor for unwanted passers-by. Eventually, the brazen young dancer opened the door in her dressing gown.

'What's the problem?' she inquired demurely.

'I have to do a cabin inspection,' Baresi replied. 'Just a routine check. May I come in?'

'I suppose so.'

The staff captain brushed her to one side with a swipe of the arm and strode into the small cabin. He could smell blood and was homing in for the kill. Eyes wide, engorged forehead veins throbbing with excitement—his prey was almost within his grasp, and boy, was he going to enjoy the next five minutes!

Scanning the room, he couldn't believe his eyes. It was empty. Where was Gambino?

'Are you alone?'

'Umm …' Claire hesitated again, and Baresi's eyes turned to the bathroom door.

'Who's in the bathroom?' he demanded.

'It's Zara, my roommate. She's sick. Had a bit of a heavy night.'

I knew Zara well. The English dancer was a tough cookie and could hold her drinks. Baresi knew Claire was lying too, and he sensed imminent victory over his wayward foe. He collected himself for a moment and moved stealthily towards the bathroom in anticipation. As he leant forward, putting his ear close to the locked door, the macabre grin of the executioner appeared across his face, and he prepared to administer the coup de grace. Suddenly, a loud shriek rang out, immediately followed by the unmistakable sound of vomiting, then splashes from the toilet bowl. Baresi recoiled in horror, promptly lost his balance, and crumpled to the floor in a heap. Claire could barely contain her laughter.

'Are you alright, Zara?' she shouted, stepping over the flailing Baresi. More retching noises came from inside, then a falsetto whimper of acknowledgement. This was indeed an Oscar-winning performance.

'She'll be okay soon,' Claire explained, giggling to herself. 'I think we'd better leave her to it.'

She ushered the bewildered staff captain back into the corridor before he came to his senses, then shut the door firmly behind him. Although he knew it was Gambino in that bathroom, Baresi also realised that it was now too late to go back and demand entry. To return and insist on witnessing the regurgitations of the innocent Zara would not look good, and he would almost certainly be dissuaded from doing so by the other officers.

He was beaten.

The Genovese's attempted coup had failed by the thinnest of margins: the width of a toilet door.

With the help of his cronies, his mistress's quick thinking, and a tactical vomit, Gambino had thwarted Baresi's plan. The awaiting deck officers shrugged their shoulders and held up their hands in response to Baresi's anguished look in that typically Italian way of expressing nonchalant resignation and feigned compassion; they knew that their master had escaped by the skin of his teeth.

Three weeks later, Baresi was transferred to another vessel.

Despite his avoidance of a fall from grace, Captain Gambino was severely rattled by this episode. For the next few weeks, he went on the warpath and became determined to settle any old scores, however minor.

On one of his Saturday morning visits to the ship, Mo gave me another of his sermons. I found it difficult to concentrate on his words, however, as my attention was distracted by his latest pilose incarnation. Pete had told me to look out for Mo's 'I've just had a haircut' hairpiece. This must have been it. The towering quiff and matted sideburns had been replaced by a shorter, neater model. Apparently, Mo dusted this specimen off every few months to give the illusion of a visit to the barber. Then, a few weeks later, he would subtly revert to his standard model.

'I hear the captain had some trouble recently, with the staff captain,' Mo began. He took another long drag on his cigarette, then stubbed out the butt. 'You see what happens? The captain has all the power, even more than me! Once he is your enemy, you must be careful.'

He nodded sagely and lit another cigarette, then continued his parable. 'I was young like you, once. Long time ago. I was very careful not to piss off the captain. If he wanted me to do something, I would say "Certainly, Captain." And if he was after a certain woman, I would leave her alone. I played The Game. I know this captain, he likes the ladies, and I know you do too. So, play The Game, Paolo; *play The Game.*'

Did Mo really know about my encounter with Gambino's 'special guest' passenger on my first night?

Maybe not, but it was clear that Mo was aware of my stoush with the master, and it was time for me to up my game.

7

SPINAL TAP AND THE CUBAN MUSCLE CRISIS

Over the next few weeks, the infirmary was quite busy, so my feud with Gambino took a back seat. Even so, my activities did not escape his eye, as he kept a vigilant watch for signs of weakness or improper behaviour. Each morning, he would call the infirmary at 8.05 am sharp on some ridiculous pretext. After the first few calls, asking if the doctor was free to give some advice on blood pressure problems (with which *all* Italians were obsessed), it was obvious that he was checking up to see if I had made it to the clinic on time. Sometimes he would send down the first officer to check the infirmary floor for stains or to see if the light bulbs needed replacing.

I made sure I gave him no cause for complaint and played Mo's Game by the book. During this period of close scrutiny, two particularly awkward medical cases presented, putting my professional skills under the microscope too.

Four hours after leaving Miami one Saturday evening, a young Guatemalan galley-hand presented himself at the crew clinic. He looked dreadful and was clearly not well. With my pidgin Spanish and the usual crew clinic sign language, I gleaned his symptoms: a severe headache since the morning, mainly at the back of the head, vomiting, and an aversion to bright light. These were classic symptoms of acute meningitis. No wonder he looked so ill. This initial impression was confirmed by my examination, which showed a high fever and neck stiffness but no other neurological complications. Without access to laboratory facilities, it would be impossible to tell between life-threatening bacterial meningitis and the more benign viral form. Technically, it could be possible to treat such a case on the ship with high-dose intravenous antibiotics, if the situation demanded, but I was in no mood to take such a risk with thirty-six hours at sea ahead of us. There was no doubt we had to get this poor chap off the ship and into a hospital as soon as possible. But we were in open sea, at least five hours from the nearest port.

I called the bridge and spoke to Captain Gambino.

'Captain, I have an emergency case. A crew member with meningitis. We must evacuate him as soon as possible.'

The captain sighed heavily. This was really bad news for him, transforming a pleasant evening's sailing into an operational nightmare. Not to mention the cost—Carnival would have to foot the bill for the evacuation of a crew member, and this played a part in the calculations too.

'Are you sure?' he replied.

'Yes. We cannot keep him onboard. What are the options?'

'Have you spoken to the hospital in Miami?'

'No. But I'll speak to them if you would prefer,' I conceded ground, remembering to play The Game.

'Yes, I think you should. To make an evacuation is a big problem for us. We must be sure.'

I went up to the bridge to make the call on the radio telephone and discussed the case with Dr Schneider at Mount Sinai Hospital in Miami.

'Sounds like a classic case, Doctor Amodeo. Get him here as soon as you can!' was his reassuring advice.

Gambino was choked.

'From our present location, it will take us five hours back to Miami. Then we have too much of the journey to make up to get to Cozumel on time,' he said, rubbing his chin thoughtfully. 'But we should still be in range for the Coastguard helicopter.'

He ordered the first officer to contact the US Coastguard Station in Miami, and they agreed upon a time and location for the rendezvous. I gave the Coastguard operator the patient's full details—name, age, height, weight, diagnosis, general condition, and blood pressure. Then I went back down to the infirmary.

The pick-up was not for another two hours, and I felt I must initiate some treatment during this hiatus. I then remembered having discovered an old microscope in the back room when I had first arrived on the ship. Having fancied myself as an exponent of medical DIY, I had ordered a Gram stain kit, with which I could make up my own specimen slides in the hope of reaching my own diagnostic conclusions. So far, though, I had only found it useful in the diagnosis of gonorrhoea, and even this was usually only an academic exercise.

But the moment of truth that my laboratory dabblings had been waiting for had arrived! If I performed a lumbar puncture on the patient, obtaining a sample of cerebrospinal fluid (CSF), I could do a quick Gram stain, pop it under the microscope, and hey presto! Confirm the presence of the deadly meningococcal bacteria and save the day. Despite the advances of modern technology, the examination of CSF from a spinal tap was still the only way of confirming a diagnosis of meningitis. This involves the insertion of a fine needle into the lower back, between two of the vertebrae, to reach the narrow sub-arachnoid space. Here lies the CSF, which surrounds the brain and spinal cord. Any infection within this space and its lining (the meninges) will show as changes in the composition of the fluid, and the presence of micro-organisms detectable by microscopy in the case of bacterial infection. In addition, it is generally good practice, if circumstances permit, to obtain all samples for bacterial culture *prior* to starting antibiotics. Otherwise, the lab may have difficulty isolating the bacteria responsible for the infection.

'Right then,' I announced to all in the infirmary, 'the helicopter will be here in two hours. In the meantime, I'm going to do a lumbar puncture.'

I explained the forthcoming proceedings to the patient as best I could.

'In dos horas venga un helicóptero. Usted vamos al hospital in Miami. Comprende?'

Spinal Tap and the Cuban Muscle Crisis

The stoic galley-hand nodded approval.

'*Ahora, yo essamina la espalda.*' I indicated his lower back.

'*Por un minuto, un poco dolor, pero solamente un minuto.*'

He seemed to understand the fact that I was about to stick a six-inch needle into his spine, and my attempts to communicate in pidgin Spanish had hopefully helped soothe his anxiety.

Before starting any procedure, making sure all the equipment was on hand and getting properly set up would be the most vital step. I always remembered the 'Six Ps', an old surgical aphorism designed to help avoid stuffing things up: *Prior Planning Prevents Piss-Poor Performance.*

I positioned the patient on the bed, laying him on his left side with knees curled up and neck bent forward, arching the spine convexly towards me. This would open up the space between the bony vertebrae. I washed my hands and donned sterile surgical gloves for the delicate procedure. First, I cleaned the skin of the lower back with antiseptic iodine solution. Then I began to inject the area between the third and fourth lumbar vertebrae, in the midline, with 1% lidocaine local anaesthetic. This is the bit that stings; after that, the area should go numb in a few minutes.

'Can I have an eighteen-gauge spinal needle, please?' I asked Kathy, who was helping me, but with a hint of suspicion in her eyes.

'Sure.' She paused for a moment, then enquired with trepidation in her voice, 'You … you have done this before, haven't you?'

'Yep. Loads. No problem.'

Which was kind of true. I had done a few, but not loads. But enough to be confident that I wasn't doing the patient a disservice. Except that I hadn't done any at sea. On a moving ship. Up until this point, I had failed to consider the fact that we were on a vessel in motion upon a non-stationary expanse of water. A sudden lilt of the ship could seriously hamper my efforts to perform the procedure without skewering the nerves leaving the spinal cord. But conditions were smooth, and it was too late to back down now.

I pushed the long needle in carefully, angling it towards the patient's bellybutton, as per textbook guidelines. A bead of sweat formed on my brow as I felt a point of resistance at about two-and-a-half inches in. This was the dura mater, the tough fibrous lining of the spinal canal. Applying firm pressure now, just momentarily, I suddenly felt the resistance give, and I stopped immediately. I was into the sub-arachnoid space. I withdrew the needle slightly, leaving just the fine plastic sheath in position, and let the CSF drip out into the collecting jar. Although it didn't display its normal vodka-like transparency, the CSF wasn't obviously cloudy and infected to the naked eye. Once a few millilitres had collected, I withdrew both needle and sheath completely, leaving nothing but a tiny needle-prick wound.

I took the specimen into the back room for examination while the nurses helped prepare our patient for his long journey. I enjoyed fiddling around in the back room with the Gram stain kit; it made me feel like a proper scientist, such as Pasteur or Fleming. But my career as a Nobel laureate was to be short-lived, as I could see no bacteria through the microscope lens. This was good news for the patient, but I was acutely aware of my lack of skill as a laboratory technician as a possible contributing factor to the negative result. Bacterial meningitis was still a possibility, so I gave a large dose of intravenous ceftriaxone, the latest kill-all antibiotic, and sent the remainder of the CSF sample with the patient for further analysis in Miami.

The pick-up time was approaching, so we moved our man in the bucket stretcher up to the aft lido deck in readiness. The rear-most portion of the deck was cleared of passengers and furniture, and the ship slowed to a crawl. Then we waited and listened for the whir of the chopper blades in the night's sky. Curious passengers peered through the windows of the adjoining Wharf Bar, and several crew members came up to watch the hazardous operation from close range. The helicopter came out of the darkness quite suddenly, the blustery wind making it difficult to hear the blades approaching. It maintained a steady altitude of just a few hundred feet as it came in over the sea, then carefully positioned itself above the open deck.

The staff captain shouted in my ear.

'It's too risky for them to land! Too windy, and the deck's too small. They are sending down a stretcher on a line. Put the patient on it!'

'Okay. No problem.'

The helicopter came down to hover at only fifty feet, matching the slow forward pace of the ship. The side door opened, and the winch man gestured for us to bring the stretcher out onto the deck, directly under the chopper. As we approached, heads bowed under the force of the helicopter's thrust, and down came the Coastguard crewman with his stretcher on a line. I gave our frightened patient a final pat on the head and 'thumbs-up' and he was transferred swiftly onto the Coastguard stretcher and tightly strapped in. Within seconds, he became airborne as the winch pulled steadily on the line, reeling our patient up to the chopper. The poor chap must have been scared stiff, dangling perilously above the ship, unable to move, with the rotor blades spinning furiously above. But in no time at all, he reached the warm belly of the helicopter, and safety. The crewman clambered aboard with him, looked down, and waved us farewell before sliding the door shut.

After all that drama, the medical team reached a unanimous decision that it had been a job well done, and we congratulated ourselves by retiring to the crew bar for the evening.

The next day, Dr Mo relayed a message from Mount Sinai Hospital. The diagnosis turned out to be the less dangerous viral form of meningitis, and the patient was doing well. My management of the case had been considered appropriate, but unsurprisingly, I was advised not to perform another spinal tap while onboard ship!

Exactly one week after the meningitis case, we were presented with an equally challenging situation. This time, though, we had left Miami far behind.

Linda called me in the officers' mess.

'Paolo, you'd better come quick. There's a passenger here with chest pain, and she doesn't look too good.'

I quickly finished off my dinner and went straight to the infirmary, just up the stairs, one deck above the mess. In the emergency bay was Mrs J: fifty-five years of age, overweight, and with the worn features of a chronic smoker. She was sat up on the bed, obviously distressed and looking pale and clammy, her breathing laboured.

'This is oxygen; it will help your breathing,' explained Linda while strapping on the mask.

'Hello. I am Doctor Amodeo. I just need to put a drip in your arm first; then we'll see what's happening, okay?'

Linda handed me the torniquet, and I tightened it around Mrs J's arm, then felt for a suitable vein at the elbow.

'What's the story?' I asked Linda.

'She was in the dining room when the chest pain started—it's been about half an hour now. Her husband says she's never had heart trouble, but she has had a few twinges this week.'

Mr J was standing close by, waiting anxiously.

'Does your wife take any regular medication?'

'Just some blood pressure tablets, little yellow ones. I can't remember the name now ... I left them in our room.'

'Don't worry, we can check later.' I tried to keep him calm while I inserted the needle into his wife's arm. 'Let me just see what's going on here, and I'll be with you shortly.'

By now, the patient's breathing had eased somewhat with the oxygen, and she seemed a little more comfortable.

'Linda, what was her BP?'

'One-forty over ninety-five. Pulse eighty-five.'

'Thanks.'

I examined her chest and found no signs of cardiac failure—the heart was still pumping effectively.

'Right, time for the ECG.'

The electrocardiogram would assess the electrical activity of the heart and tell us if she was having angina or a full-blown heart attack (myocardial infarct, MI). We positioned the electrodes, one to each of the four limbs and six across the front of the chest, and connected the leads to the machine. The fine trace came out on the graph paper, and not surprisingly, it showed typical changes of an acute MI.

'Hmm. ST elevation in leads II, III and aVf. Looks like an inferior MI.'

The ECG indicated damage to the lower-most part of the heart muscle, but the patient's general condition was reasonably good, indicating that the area involved was probably limited and not compromising the heart's action too much.

'Linda, we'll need to give her some morphine. Can you draw some up please?'

'Sure, Paolo. Coming right up.'

I explained the situation to our patient and Mr J.

'Mrs J, I'm afraid to say that it looks like you are having a heart attack. But the good news is that your heart is still working well. I'll give you a shot for the pain now.' And I indicated the syringe of morphine that Linda had passed to me.

'Then it's really a matter of keeping a close eye on you, as your condition is quite stable now. I think you'll be fine.' I pushed the tip of the syringe into the 'bung' on the cannula. 'This will ease the pain.'

I gauged the response as I pushed slowly on the syringe. Bit by bit, her pain lessened, and after a few minutes, I was able to cease the injection.

'That's ten milligrams, for the record. Let's give her three hundred milligrams of aspirin and keep the oxygen on.'

'Sure,' replied Linda. 'I'll hook her up to the cardiac monitor.'

The main danger now would be a ventricular arrhythmia, an abnormal heart rhythm resulting from a disruption of the electrical conduction pathways of the heart. Some arrhythmias can be quite benign, but those developing immediately following an MI are usually more sinister. Hence the monitor to pick them up early and treat with appropriate intravenous drugs. The more dramatic ones, like ventricular fibrillation, where the rhythm deteriorates into completely chaotic electrical activity, would set the heart quivering uselessly and manifest as a cardiac arrest. This would require the use of a defibrillator to get it going again.

So ideally, this patient should be in a coronary care unit, and not the ms *Lucky Star* infirmary, I concluded.

I went up to discuss the case with the captain. The bridge was in darkness, save for the soft footlights and glowing navigational instruments. It was an awful night outside.

Visibility was low, and rain lashed against the large windows spanning the front of the bridge. The first officer kept a careful watch at the helm. I found the captain in his quarters, and this time, he respected my professional opinion without question.

However, the master was still a little perturbed 'But now we are too far from Miami, the Coastguard cannot reach us here.'

He took me back to the bridge and showed me on the map.

'We have come through the Strait of Florida,' he explained, pointing to the blue bit between the southern tip of Florida and the large island of Cuba, 'and soon we shall sail around the eastern tip of Cuba and head due west to Cozumel.'

'So where does that leave us?'

'Well, Doctor, it's a bad position. We can't stop off in Cuba! How is the patient?'

'She's stable at the moment, but we have to get her off the ship, there's no question. There's a chance she could run into serious trouble with her heart between here and Cozumel. You understand?'

He understood.

When it came to passengers falling seriously ill at sea under the care of the company, the priority was to get them to a hospital as soon as possible. This was done not only to fast-track their medical care but also to reduce the chance of an onboard catastrophe. The passenger's medical/travel insurance would take care of the evacuation, and a death onboard had to be avoided at all costs—that would not be a good look for a cruise company.

Gambino thought for a moment, then called the radio room and spoke to Santos.

'Can you get me the naval base at Guantanamo? We have a medical case.'

I was unaware that USA had any presence on Castro's island of Cuba, but apparently the US Navy had stationed a base there for almost a hundred years. They agreed to send out a boat to pick up Mrs J, so the *Lucky Star* changed course and headed for what was technically Cuban waters.

On reaching the agreed map reference point, the cruise ship slowed. The approaching Navy boat appeared as a fast-moving blip on the radar screen, approaching from the west. As it closed in, visual contact was made through the driving rain, and the vessel turned and slowed, taking up a position parallel to the *Lucky Star*, fifty yards off the starboard side. We waited anxiously by the crew gangway door with Mrs J wrapped up in blankets and waterproofs in her wheelchair. Her condition had remained stable, but I became seriously concerned about the risk of causing further stress on her heart when I surveyed the developing scene outside.

The Navy vessel was gradually edging its way towards the *Lucky Star*, hoping to come alongside, close enough to make a simple transfer. But the weather conditions were making this manoeuvre extremely difficult. The staff captain bellowed instructions with a megaphone from the doorway while ropes were slung between the ships at either end to steady them. The swell pushed the two ships together for a moment, then away again, as the small Navy boat bobbed its way closer with each cycle.

I looked over at Linda; she was biting her lip.

'Looks pretty scary out there,' I said.

'Yeah. I wouldn't fancy being transferred across there—it's enough to give *anyone* a heart attack!'

Fortunately, our conversation was out of earshot of the poor Mrs J.

Linda grabbed my arm and pulled me in close.

'Be careful when you go over. Pete nearly got killed one time.'

'What?'

'When I was on the *Celebration*, Pete was transferring a patient, and he slipped. Pierre the security chief grabbed his arm and stopped him from falling between the two boats. Would have been crushed, ay.'

I gulped and watched the Navy boat approach the *Lucky Star*. It was making steady progress sideways and was now within twenty feet, but it was swinging alarmingly up and down with each wave. My stomach began to do the same.

'You mean I have to go across there?' I remarked in horror.

'Yeah, it looks like it, ay. They'll put a kind of bridge thing across, and you must take the patient over. And don't forget to come back!'

'Bloody hell!'

Suddenly, the Navy boat smashed against the door frame on another upward lurch.

The staff captain screamed into the radio, '*It's no good! It's too rough. Back away! Back away!*'

He waved frantically out of the door, gesturing at the Navy crew to go back some. They too realised it would not work; there was too much vertical motion for the transfer to be done, so the boat's engine powered up and steered it away a little.

The Navy suggested another way.

'We'll throw a line and pulley over. Secure the patient to the chair on the pulley and we'll reel her in.'

'Okay! Throw the line up to the aft deck,' instructed the staff captain.

We were told to go up to the aft lido deck and wait for him. The boats moved close again, and the line was handed over to the awaiting deckhands. By the time we reached the deck, the line had been secured. It stretched from a sturdy metal column fixture above our heads, over the turbulent thirty feet of sea between the two vessels, and down to the Navy boat.

Without further ado, the trembling Mrs J was securely strapped into the small chair and attached to the line. The staff captain signalled over to the Navy crew with a wave of his hand and yelled down the radio, *'Okay, good to go!'*

I could only imagine what was going through the mind of our distraught patient as the pulley began to slide along the line towards the Navy vessel. The chair bobbed and swayed its way down off the aft deck, hanging precariously over the rough seas below. The moment transported me into Edgar Allan Poe's terrifying short story *A Descent into the Maelstrom*, triggering disturbing visions of a powerful, swirling vortex rising from the tempestuous Cuban waters and devouring the helpless Mrs J.

There was nothing we could do now. The rain continued to lash as we looked on in disbelief and crossed our fingers that all would go well. The Navy crew summoned all their strength to pull her in as quickly as possible, and each lurch of the chair sent our tell-tale hearts pounding with the stress of witnessing this agonising scene before us.

But thankfully, and to our great relief, the operation was a success as Mrs J reached the US Navy ship without further incident to be whisked away to the safety of Guantanamo Naval Base. We all thanked the gods and hoped that Mrs J and her beleaguered heart muscle would survive her very own Cuban crisis.

After visibly doing a good job over those difficult few weeks, I felt that I had garnered a healthy respect for my work as the ship's doctor. I also realised that I was in the unique position of being the only senior officer who was not on a hard-earned maritime career pathway—to me, this job was a *break* from my career, a working holiday. So, if Gambino continued with his vendetta, so be it. I now had the confidence and courage to withstand anything he could throw at me, and I was willing to take a few bullets in the name of adventure.

I began to liken myself to one of my historical heroes, TE Lawrence, the British WWI army colonel. He was known for his stoic and gallant character and his rebellious attitude towards the inflexible military machine. I also admired his eccentric mindset, which was well summed up by an early scene in David Lean's magnificent movie *Lawrence of Arabia*.

After lighting a colleague's cigarette, Lawrence allows the match to burn all the way down to his fingertips before snuffing it out. Having witnessed the stunt, his associate attempts it himself, only to blow out the match before it gets anywhere close to burning down to his own fingers.

'That damn well hurts!' he states, barely concealing his amazement.

'Certainly, it hurts,' replies the cool and calm Lawrence.

'Well, what's the trick then?'

'The trick ... is not *minding* that it hurts.'

THE DEVIL AND THE DEEP BLUE SEA

About a week later, Mo told me that Guy was taking a short break from the *Tropicale* and would be passing through Miami. I hadn't seen Guy since he passed the baton over to me on the *Carnivale* about five months ago, so I was very excited when I arranged to meet up for lunch with one of the Bates Street Boys.

We met up at Hooters, near the Port of Miami, well known for its delicious snow crabs and attractive, scantily clad waitresses. I told Guy of my recent medical cases.

Guy commented, 'Wow, I can't believe you did a lumbar puncture on a moving ship! That must have been tricky.'

'Well, you know I've always liked a good challenge.'

'Yep, spot on, Paolo,' Guy replied, raising his beer. 'You know, I had a really challenging case a few weeks ago on the *Tropicale*. We had a young woman with out-of-control epilepsy. It was pretty scary, having to deal with that on the ship, but at least I had great help from the nurses and the security chief.'

Josh Maldito was six foot seven inches tall. He was lean, mean, and had a menacing face, amplified by a sardonic smile that revealed a single gold tooth in place of an upper incisor, a remnant of his previous life sparring in the boxing clubs of South-West Chicago. Pensioned out of the police force after sustaining a back injury while tackling a pimp, he had moved into the security business. At the age of thirty-six, he found himself as the new chief security officer on the ms *Tropicale*. For him, this was a good thing, as without the protection of a uniform, his life would undoubtedly have been one long fight against people who didn't appreciate his acerbic wit. Luckily, Guy had the same dry sense of humour, so they hit it off immediately.

Josh first came into Guy's world holding a tea towel around the bleeding forearm that he had cuffed to his own. That forearm belonged to Miguel, a spindly cleaner from Guatemala. Guy had been summoned to the galley, where Miguel had used his arm to defend himself against a twelve-inch kitchen knife wielded by Juan, a compatriot galley-hand. But the moustachioed Juan was in no position to make an escape, as Miguel had pushed him backwards into a large vat of steaming hot soup during the fracas. Juan suffered third-degree burns to his legs, buttocks, and scrotum and was already being administered some analgesia by Isabella, the Costa Rican nurse who was first on the scene. Fortunately, she spoke fluent Spanish, which saved Josh and Guy a lot of extra work.

It transpired that Juan and Miguel had both been thrown out of their home in Guatemala by the village elders, as they kept fighting over the local princess. Both sought a life at sea, but fate had thrown them back together on the ms *Tropicale*.

Fortunately, Miguel only needed a few stitches to his arm, but he spent an uncomfortable night in the brig before being summarily despatched, without investigation or appeal, at the next port of call, St Thomas. The badly burned Juan spent an even more uncomfortable night in the infirmary before suffering a similar fate via the emergency department in Charlotte Amalie. The company wouldn't tolerate any ill discipline; if you were punched, you had got yourself into a situation, so you were dismissed too.

One glorious Saturday afternoon in Old San Juan, there was a commotion when a group of seventy-two evangelists from New Jersey stepped aboard the *Tropicale* and began an impromptu gospel concert in the ship's atrium. It was like a scene from a musical—in fact, Guy looked over the stairwell, trying to spot James Brown or John Belushi. It was clear that this was a happy crowd, and it was also obvious that the F&B manager might not have stocked up quite enough for this particular cruise. The only member of the group that was not morbidly obese was the rector. Fortunately, the Hooters had been cruising the week before, so there were some leftovers in the kitchen. However, the infirmary condom supply was gossamer thin.

Early next Tuesday morning, as they sailed from Grenada to Venezuela, Guy was called urgently by Isabella to a passenger's room. It was one of the downstairs, inside cabins that had only been added because there was an unused internal space by one of the flues. Even if the cabin cost nothing to rent, the passenger would probably eat and drink a few hundred bucks' worth on a week-long cruise. Carnival made sure it squeezed every possible dollar of profit from every corner of the ship.

In that tiny space, Guy found one of the evangelical 'sisters' in dire straits. She was suffering from continuous seizures, a condition known as status epilepticus. A known epileptic, she had decided that she didn't need to take her anti-seizure medication, as she would be 'relaxing' on the cruise. Of course, when the levels dropped by day four, she ended up in a life-threatening situation. Nobody knew how long she had been fitting for, and it was possible that she had already suffered brain damage from lack of oxygen. Sister Grace was only twenty-three years old. She was around five foot four and had somehow managed to gorge herself to the biblical size of about 420 lbs (190 kg).

The immediate imperative was to gain intravenous access in order to stop the seizures. This task was not going to be easy, especially in listing seas; it was like playing darts blindfolded.

After eight attempts, Guy managed to hit a deeply hidden blood vessel, and they all celebrated in relief on nailing the bullseye. The magic recipe of a few ounces of skill, one can of steady nerves, and a mountain of luck had saved the day. Guy quickly injected an industrial dose of intravenous diazepam, and Sister Grace stopped fitting.

But they were not out of the woods yet. Their patient was no longer convulsing, but she was still deeply unconscious.

'Right. So far, so good,' Guy announced, 'but we must get her to the infirmary and secure her airway. She might need intubating. Isabella, how many portable oxygen cylinders do we have?'

'Just the one. That's about thirty minutes' worth. And we've already used half of it.'

'Shit. Right, Josh, we need to organise a stretcher team and get her out of here ASAP!'

'Sure, Doc. They're on their way now,' Josh reassured them from his position just outside the narrow doorway.

Two stewards turned up carrying a stretcher with wooden poles, but on seeing the huge size of the comatose patient, they immediately turned around without uttering a word and sped back down the stairs. A few minutes later, they reappeared with two mates and a heavier-duty stretcher with aluminium poles. They managed to roll the canvas under her and the poles through the holes, but due to the dimensions of the room and particularly the cabin door, the casualty was too wide to fit through lying on her back.

She was still unrousable, so Isabella continued to assist her shallow breathing by ventilating with a bag and mask attached to the oxygen cylinder.

Josh concentrated on resolving the difficult logistics of escaping the now feverish cabin, voicing his concerns into the radio.

'We need two more stewards; four's not going to be enough. And get the first officer down here; we must try and remove the door.'

The first officer subsequently brought down a crowbar and some heavy-duty tools. But it was no good; the door just wouldn't budge.

Guy realised they would have to try another method.

'Okay. Let's sit her up. Isabella, keep her chin up and keep bagging her. When she's sat up, we'll have to try and squash in her sides and try to shuffle her through the door.'

The stewards tried to mould her rolls of flab as they attempted to steer Sister Grace through the doorway, inch by inch.

By this time, a selection of the gospel choir and the rector had gathered in the corridor. One of the worried onlookers called out.

'This can't be the right way to get a casualty out of a cabin!'

The rector solemnly repeated, 'Yes, this can't be the right way to get a casualty out of a cabin.'

This was followed by several other members of the congregation muttering exactly the same phrase. It was easy to see why they were a good choir. This was shortly followed by a harmonious chorus of 'Is this the right way to get a casualty out of the cabin?'.

Before the next infinitesimal wave of repetition began, the rector stepped in again.

'Yes, *Doctor,* is this the right way to get a casualty out of a cabin?'

Guy was in no position to answer. Stressed about the possibility of losing the intravenous access, Guy was muffled somewhere between rolls of fat that could have been anywhere from the thigh to the breast, clinging on to the drip. The stewards continued to slap the flab in order to get her through the eye of this needle. If only she was a camel!

Fortunately, Josh came to Guy's aid. He put his hand up and announced to the madding crowd, 'Hold on, hold on. I've got it right here …'

He reached for the flip-top notebook in his shirt pocket and theatrically thumbed through several pages while the awaiting audience held its breath in anticipation.

Josh smiled towards the rector, revealing his single gold tooth, which shone like a burning bush.

'Yes! Here it is! Page forty of the *Mariners Emergency Guide: How to Evacuate a Hippopotamus from a Shoebox*! Let's see. Hmm … yes … yes. We are following the guidelines to the letter, sir!'

This immediately put a stop to the waves of sanctimonious fervour, and Guy buried his head further into the rolls of fat to conceal his laughter. A few more shoves and wiggles later, they finally made it through the door with the moribund stretcher-case. Two more stewards were summoned, and eight of them carried the heavy load down the two flights of stairs to the infirmary, but only just. The stretcher had buckled. It turned out the aluminium tubes were, of course, hollow.

The medical team stabilised Sister Grace in the infirmary, but Guy was still worried that the cannula might fall out. He was fearful that he may not be able to get another drip in, and that thought made Guy sit in a ridiculously overprotective vigil for the next few hours. Whatever her comorbidities, she was only twenty-three. Guy was twenty-six. If he hadn't got a vein, he would have already outlived her.

Two hours later, the *Tropicale* docked in La Guira, near Caracas, and the patient was disembarked via ambulance to the local hospital. The whole episode got Guy a bit rattled, so once Sister Grace was off the ship, he went to his favourite South American restaurant for an early lunch and tried to relax a bit.

After his refreshing time-out, Guy slowly walked back to the ship, happy that Sister Grace had survived and relieved that they had avoided a death onboard. As he approached the gangplank, Josh was there to meet him.

'Hi, Josh. Man, that was a near miss. What's up?'

Josh was still looking very serious despite their team victory. 'The boss wants a chat.'

'What do you mean?'

'There's still a problem with these religious people. The captain wants to see you.'

Guy made his way up to the bridge, wondering what could possibly be wrong. The captain guided him into his office and closed the door behind them.

'Dottore, we have a problem with these Evangeliste. They are many. Very important for the company. They have phoned head office and insist that their "sister" is back onboard for the cruise back Stateside. They are very unhappy for her to stay in Venezuela.'

'What? Do they know she's lucky to be alive?'

'Yes, they know that. But they are quite serious about this. And I don't want to cause trouble with them.'

Guy had to control his anger and calm himself down.

'Captain, let me talk to them. I'll explain that she is much safer in the hospital having her anti-convulsive levels boosted and then flying back home when it's safe for her to do so.'

'Okay, good luck. But we pull rope in three hours.'

Guy hadn't factored in the power of God or the dogma of the rector, but he was determined to resolve the issue. The rector and his entourage were not hard to find. Guy explained the situation, but the rector's reply had him even more perplexed.

'Hallelujah! The Lord has saved her, working through you. And she will be saved again; praise be the Lord!'

'So, what if I can't access a vein?'

'The Lord will see you through!' the rector prophesised, looking up and raising both arms to the heavens.

'And if he doesn't?'

'Then that is His choice for Sister Grace.'

His loyal followers then burst into chorus, 'Praise be the Lord!'

Guy was struggling to find a crack in the rector's divine armour. Scratching his head, he pondered which route to take next. It would have to be Route 666: explicitly lay out the worst-case scenario and leave no room for debate.

'So, you are prepared to let a twenty-three-year-old die for the sake of three days on a cruise ship?'

'If that is His will,' replied the unwavering rector.

'Praise be the Lord!' the chorus rang out once again.

This went on for some time. These religious zealots clearly had no sense of reality, and they had reached a confounding impasse.

Guy went back to see the captain again.

'Captain, these people are mad! It is patently unsafe for her to travel. I have cleared it with a neurologist at Mount Sinai, and the medical director. She needs to stay in hospital and be flown home when medically stable. We cannot let her continue on this cruise.'

'Dottore, they are a very important and large group on this ship. I have told the rector that she can continue with them home.'

This was now getting unbelievable. How could the captain not see the seriousness of her condition? He was an intelligent man, but he had placed Guy somewhere between the Devil and the Deep Blue Sea.

Considering his options, Guy recounted his Hippocratic Oath—*First, do no harm.* He realised that if Sister Grace was onboard for the next thirty-six hours at sea, it would totally be his responsibility if she died. That could lead to a General Medical Council hearing in the UK and possible manslaughter charges in the US. But a medical incident at sea could be far more complicated. Within three miles of land, it would come under local jurisdiction, so on their next run past several small islands, this could be the USA, the UK, France, the Netherlands, or Venezuela. Further out at sea, international maritime law applied. It would be very difficult to prosecute anyone through the American, Italian,

Liberian, or British courts, which was why the captain was, in essence, *Judge Dredd*. But for serious cases on an American-owned ship, the FBI could also get involved.

Guy also knew that according to international maritime law, it was illegal for a cruise ship to sail without a doctor or a radio officer onboard.

What was he to do?

After taking his time deliberating how to handle this burning question, he saw the light. It became crystal clear that Guy's decision would have to be based purely on professional integrity.

Guy changed into his officer's uniform and walked back into his favourite bar to buy a six-pack of San Miguel. In full view of the ship's bridge, he positioned himself at the quayside, sat down, and opened a beer. It was now around five o'clock, and the *Tropicale* was due to sail soon.

A few minutes later, a deckhand came down off the ship to receive his message.

It was simple.

'Captain, you can sail with either Sister Grace or me, but not both.'

Guy kept his head low for the rest of the cruise, and the captain never chastised him, nor did he thank him. But secretly he knew Guy was right, and his professional deference to him was clear from the very next captain's meeting when, after every department head had summarised their week, the captain wound up the meeting to hoots of laughter from his obsequious apostles. 'Thank you everyone. Now, if the dottore would be good enough to let me know when I can set sail ...'

Guy's challenging tale emphasised his great medical skills, plus his assertiveness to deal with a captain who had put the ship's doctor in a very difficult position.

The story also reminded me of my one and only religious experience. Every year in the run-up to Christmas, Sheffield Medical School held its annual Four-Legged Fancy Dress Pub Crawl. Each team of three people, with legs tied to each other's, would try to outrace the other groups from pub-to-pub along West Street, ending up at a party in the mess. One year, I got together with two female friends, who dressed up as nuns. That left me with no choice but to don a pair of sandals and a long, curly white wig and beard fashioned from bundles of cottonwool and some sticky tape. The inscription on the front of my pure white cloak left no doubt as to my identity: *I Am God, So Sod Off!*

Later on, at the afterparty, divine providence intervened and led me to an unholy match-up with an immaculate student pharmacist by the name of Mary!

9
GOING DOWN

The island of Cozumel lies in the Western Caribbean, just off Mexico's Yucatan peninsula. The island itself is not known for its beauty, consisting mostly of flat mangrove swamps and a few decent beaches. The main attraction of Cozumel lies in the crystal-blue waters in which it sits, for just offshore can be found some of the most beautiful coral reefs in the world. Ever since the great undersea explorer Jacques Cousteau revealed the treasures of the Palancar Reef in 1961, Cozumel had become one of the most visited scuba diving sites on the planet, rivalling Australia's Great Barrier Reef and the Red Sea.

The ms *Lucky Star* docked at Cozumel every Monday morning, so this gave me an excellent opportunity to take scuba lessons and become a certified open-water diver. I teamed up with Zara and some of the gift shop staff, David, Lucy, and Sandra, and ventured into the deep. I found scuba diving to be enormously pleasurable and good for the soul. Once past the initial feelings of anxiety and claustrophobia, one becomes magically transported into another world, one of peace and freedom. I used to love watching the TV series

The Undersea World of Jacques Cousteau as a teenager, as the famous frogman took us on his latest adventure: deep into an undersea cave to visit his favourite prehistoric monstrosity, or perhaps to simply join him in the humble pleasures of swimming with the wonderful dolphins.

I had never been particularly interested in the sea, nor sailing, but the simple tranquillity and grace experienced underwater was both relaxing and awe inspiring. From the simple sponges swaying silently in the current, and the rays of sunlight refracted by streams of glittering bubbles, to the most spectacular and bizarrely shaped fish, they amaze, they inspire, and they bestow a calmness and serenity to the mind.

One of the most thrilling experiences around is surely to dive at night for the first time. Waiting on the boat at twilight, that most mischievous time of day, when the vermilion sky plays tricks on your eyes and the sea transforms into a luxuriously tempting ultraviolet milk bath. Flashlight on, ready to go. Then dive under just as the violet glow darkens. With some light at the surface and a buddy close by, there appears no cause for concern until you begin to descend. With each foot down and each minute that passes, the twilight turns to night and the sea blackens, and all you can see are the flashlights close by and your hand in front of your mask. A good, responsible dive master is especially important here, as it is easy to become disorientated, claustrophobic, or lost. One glance into the blackness behind is enough to convince that sticking together is of paramount importance—there could have been a man-eating giant squid breathing down my neck, but I would never have spotted it.

So don't look back; follow the flashlights! The sense of mystery and adventure was wonderful, and the darkness awakened the strangest of creatures: loutish lobsters scuffling around kicking sand in each other's face; moray eels leaping from their rocky hideout like banditos on the mountain pass; and maybe a giant squid (don't look back now). On reaching the surface at the end of the dive, the exhilaration was overwhelming, and the overall feeling among us first-timers was unforgettable. And after that incredible experience, all it took was one beer to send us all into space.

Around this time, there was also a dark side to the dive community in Cozumel. Our divemaster, Tony, the ship's DJ, told us about an exclusive group amongst the local macho dive community, known as the 200 Club. Membership was limited to those stupid (and lucky) enough to have dived to two hundred feet and survived. In recreational diving, anything between sixty to one-hundred-and-twenty feet is considered a deep dive, and to venture much deeper than this requires special equipment, helium-mix tanks, and a thoroughly professional attitude. The physics of diving to such a depth with only regular equipment makes the macho endeavour of reaching two hundred feet tantamount to suicide. If nitrogen narcosis didn't get you, then decompression sickness probably would. Not that these guys cared; they were cool and invincible. But every month or so, we would hear about the latest to perish while attempting to join the 200 Club.

Many happy days were spent in Cozumel, every Monday for four months: diving, lazing around the beaches, or exploring the island in an open-top VW Beetle. The place revolved around tourism, and there wasn't much in the way of Mexican culture on offer, but the locals were warm and always happy to see us. One favourite lunch spot was Ernesto's, a friendly hangout near the port, which served the best sizzling beef fajitas around. After a morning dive, we would lounge around Ernesto's outdoor terrace to relax and indulge in the array of spicy dishes on offer.

One particular speciality was not on the menu, however, and a nod and a wink was usually all that was needed to make the order, usually when it was someone's birthday or suchlike. The knowing waiter would scurry into the bar and return with a bottle of tequila, some Sprite, and a motorcycle crash helmet. The hapless victim soon became surrounded by the entire restaurant staff as he was strapped into the helmet and prepared to experience Ernesto's Tequila Head Slammer. One waiter would steady the helmeted head, tipping it backwards, as another simultaneously poured the tequila and Sprite into the mouth from a theatrical height. The whole restaurant held its breath as the critical moment approached, and just when the tequila and Sprite mixture began to overflow, the victim's head would be violently shaken from side to side before he was given a chance to swallow. The effect was like drinking a small incendiary device while diving headlong into a food mixer. Do not try this at home.

Lazy Mexican days inevitably deteriorated into a tequila-fuelled frenzy at Carlos 'N Charlies, the liveliest bar in

Cozumel where tourists, passengers, crew, staff, and officers cavorted freely in a sea of inebriation. You could not buy a bottle of beer here; they came only in an ice bucket of six or ten. Tequila was served by a team of mobile banditos who expertly poured from the calf-skin cask while standing on the table. This was not a place to take your mother. The place reached fever pitch as midnight approached and the unique effects of the tequila took a grip. Music pumped and bodies lurched and staggered in the melee. Finally, the casualties were rounded up and poured into taxis back to the ship for more punishment at the deck party.

Tequila is strange stuff indeed. Anyone who has ever touched the stuff will have their own story to tell and will attest to the often-psychotic state of drunkenness achieved. It's not actually hallucinogenic, though, and doesn't contain any psychoactive substances other than ethanol. But it does have that strange reputation, similar to absinthe or moonshine.

One Sunday night at around 2 am, I received a call in my room. I was a bit worse for wear, but as always, I sobered up quickly with the call to duty.

'Doc, you awake?' It was Charlie, our chief of security.

'Yeah, just about. What's up?'

'Some guy has gone psycho. We're not sure what's wrong with him, but it's taken four men to pin him down.'

'What do you mean psycho?' I asked.

'Well, he was found on a stairwell in a crew area below deck. He had a fire going! Then he went crazy and attacked one of my guards. We have him pinned down in the marshalling area; can you come and take a look?'

'Sure. Sounds a bit strange. Can you find out more, maybe from friends or family? I'll meet you there.'

'Okay, see you down there, Doc.'

Charlie didn't mess around. He was a retired New York cop in his late fifties who had seen it all, and he wasn't fazed by anything. So, if the chief needed my help, I was there without question. I threw on my uniform, picked up my emergency medical bag, and headed for the marshalling area, two decks below. This was the largest space below deck, and it was used for the delivery and storage of shoreside supplies. It was big enough for a couple of forklift trucks to work in and spanned two decks in height. I found the maniac in the centre of this floorspace, held down by four security guards, one on each limb. He looked young, maybe eighteen years of age, his shirt was torn, and his feet were bare. He was lying quietly with eyes closed.

I knelt down and spoke to him.

'Hello. I am the ship's doctor. What's your name? Are you alright?'

The questions seemed futile, but I had to give the guy a chance. His reply was garbled rubbish. He began to thrash, eyes popping demonically from his contorted face. From his mouth came the most bizarre combination of impossible words, together with a barrage of spit and primitive grunts. The guards managed to hold him down until he became quiet again, but not before he had scared the hell out of me. If I didn't know any better, I'd have guessed he was possessed by the Devil and speaking in tongues.

But maybe he was a schizophrenic experiencing an acute psychotic episode? I'd seen these before, people utterly convinced that they were being taken over by an evil force, or perhaps aliens, and that everyone was out to get them. Most schizophrenics in the throes of an acute psychotic crisis that I had come across were either terrified or terrifying. Or both.

I performed a perfunctory examination as best I could. There were no external signs of a head injury, nor alcohol on his breath. His pupils were both reactive to light and equal in response. Pulse and blood pressure were both normal too.

'Let's check his blood sugar. I need to do a pinprick on his finger.'

One of the guards positioned a suitable finger while I reached in my bag for the glucose test kit. It could be that he was a diabetic; a very low blood sugar from too much insulin could cause confused and aggressive behaviour. It was 130 mg/dl, which was normal.

I couldn't figure this out.

'What do you reckon?' I asked one of the guards.

'Seems crazy to me, Doc!'

'What happened though?'

'I found him on the stairway on Deck Three, making a fire; he had matches and paper and some rags. I had to put the fire out first, so he had time to run off.'

'But you found him again?'

'Yep. I called for help, and we searched for him. Santos found him in the officers' mess. He was trying to set fire to the table setting.'

'What? In the mess!'

The mess was two doors away from my cabin! And a fire onboard a vessel at sea was a most alarming prospect and potentially the most dangerous scenario of them all (except for icebergs and giant squid).

The guard continued his disturbing recount. 'He was crazy! He attacked Santos with a bottle, but we got there in time.'

As I pondered my next move, Charlie came down and threw some light on the situation.

'I've just spoken to some of his buddies. This guy has been drinking tequila all day!'

'So, he's just drunk?'

'Yeah. Just,' Charlie replied, rolling his eyes.

'Really? No shit! Well, if that's the case, then he's all yours, Charlie!'

I then remembered seeing a couple of straitjackets in an infirmary cupboard. They had looked brand new, and I was dying to try them out. This seemed like the perfect opportunity.

'Good idea,' said Charlie. 'This loony is dangerous; we can't have the guy running round setting fire to the ship. Goddammit, let's put him in the brig.'

The chief was always on the lookout for a bit of action, so I wasn't going to spoil his fun. Besides, he had a point; this guy had lost the plot. Charlie pulled out his notebook and made a short entry: *Zero-two twenty hours. Arsonist checked by doctor. No medical problems.*

This was the notorious jotter he would pull from his top pocket when facing a security issue worthy of his attention.

He would grip his stubby little HB pencil tightly near the tip and, in a momentary break from chewing his gum, lick the pencil tip twice while he collected his thoughts. It was easy to envisage him on the streets of New York, chewing his gum and swinging his night-stick as he pounded the beat, stopping to book Johnny Foreigner for jaywalking and reaching for *that* pencil. Each time I saw him write in his notebook and lick the pencil, the surer I was that he would soon display the first symptoms of chronic lead poisoning; if only I knew what they were.

Between six of us, we eventually managed to strap the young whirling dervish into the straitjacket, but only after three rounds of all-in wrestling and a few nifty country dancing manoeuvres. I was intrigued to find that the ship's brig was a small, padded cell, eight feet square, with a barred window and huge bolt on the heavy door.

'This'll do nicely,' Charlie enthused as we bundled the crazed drunkard into the brig.

The next day, I awoke to find out that the prisoner had not only managed to extricate himself from the straitjacket but had torn the cell to shreds in an inebriated frenzy. But by morning, he had sobered up enough to be escorted to the bridge for an interview with the captain. His parents were naturally distraught to hear about their son's wild antics, but it transpired that this was not the first time he had become a crazed lunatic after drinking tequila. The captain explained that it would not be prudent to let their son remain onboard ship, as he was a danger to himself and the whole vessel. They reluctantly agreed, and he was escorted off the ship forthwith to make his own way home from Cozumel.

Strange stuff, that tequila.

On 24th August 1992, the south-east coast of Florida was hit by a Category 5 storm, Hurricane Andrew. It was the most powerful storm to make landfall in USA in decades, and it caused widespread devastation south of Miami. A state of emergency was declared in Dade County, thousands lost their homes, and sixty-five people were killed.

Fortunately, the *Lucky Star* had left the Port of Miami two days before the strike, and other ships were sent to sea to avoid them being pummelled against the pier by the high winds. When the hurricane had passed, the ms *Ecstasy* returned to port and was used as temporary accommodation for company employees who had found themselves homeless. News of the disaster filtered through to us in Cozumel, and all were anxious to hear from friends and relatives in our home port. Thankfully, the number of casualties had been minimised by the advance hurricane warnings and evacuations, so all concerned were reported safe.

This good news cheered us and enabled the celebration of the other auspicious occasion on this date to continue unabashed. Plans had been made to mark my twenty-sixth birthday with a beach party, followed by cocktails in my cabin after we set sail.

As a rule, cabin parties were illegal.

The ship's regulations stated that a gathering of more than three people in one's quarters constituted a party, so a legal celebration was technically out of the question. Nevertheless, Robert, Linda, and Zara helped me prepare my room, which involved little more than filling the small fridge with alcohol and plugging in the stereo system. My cabin was not that big, but it had room enough to contain a double bed, a small desk, and a wardrobe, with an ensuite bathroom attached. A round porthole set in the wall above the bed allowed in some light and gave an ocean view of sorts, but only just above sea-level.

If we kept the numbers and the music down, there shouldn't be any trouble, we thought. However, this proved to be a most naïve assumption, and had I stopped for a moment to consider my previous track record for hosting wild parties, I might have avoided the calamity that ensued.

Back in the Bristol Royal Infirmary (BRI), I volunteered to organise the Doctors' Mess Christmas Party towards the end of my six-month stint at the hospital. I arranged the usual party essentials: sound system, disco lighting, drinks for the bar, and a poster publicity campaign. I also had a secret weapon up my sleeve: my Madchester Mixtape, a compilation of the latest indie-pop and house tunes I had brought down from my previous job in Manchester, which I thought could unleash something beyond the 'usual'. So, I also rented out state-of-the-art laser lighting and some smoke machines to add extra atmosphere to the event.

By midnight, the party was in full flow, and the Madchester Mix was indeed cooking up a storm of epic proportions; the ground-breaking music and club-like atmosphere were a big hit with the crowd. The mess was rocking.

But then suddenly something put a stop to proceedings—the fire alarms started ringing out. Initially, most of the partygoers ignored it and carried on drinking and dancing, but ten minutes later, five fire engines turned up, the mess was invaded by a dozen firefighters in full gear, and the BRI started evacuation procedures for its four hundred inpatients.

Only then did I realise that I had forgotten to tape up the smoke detectors, and the alarm had been instantly relayed to the local fire department. I had failed to implement the mantra of the 'Six Ps', and in the process, I gained the notorious handle of MC Docski, The Banned DJ.

'How many are coming, do you think?' Robert asked me as he put down a case of rum he had purloined from the ship's bar stocks.

'Well, let's see. There's us four and Kathy, the five Shoppies. Who else is there?'

I couldn't remember who would be working at the deck party that night.

Zara helped the count. 'Some of the casino guys said they'd be down in between shifts.'

'And Giovanni the electrician,' added Linda coyly.

We had been careful not to invite all and sundry, particularly those with close ties to the bridge, unless Linda fancied them, of course.

'Okay, that makes about fifteen, tops. That should be fine, not too messy. Right, who's for a cocaine shooter?' I suggested with glee.

Zara reached into the fridge, pulling out the relevant bottles, grinning mischievously.

'You guys are evil,' Linda complained. 'We'll all be unconscious before the bloody thing starts!'

We all laughed heartily at this not unlikely scenario. Then Robert carefully poured four cocaine shooters while we looked on, admiring his well-honed bartending skills.

'Cheers, Rob,' I said, raising my glass.

'Let's wish you a happy birthday while we can still talk straight, ay,' Linda suggested, raising her own drink.

'Happy birthday, Doctor Death!' exclaimed Zara.

'Here's to a good party!' Rob added with his usual boyish giggle of anticipation.

Two hours later, my cabin was awash with partygoers. Zara poured another rum and coke as we surveyed the scene.

'I never imagined so many people could fit in here,' she said.

'What did you say?' I was straining to hear her above the thumping Madchester Mixtape.

'There must be thirty people in here!'

We had passed the point of no return long ago, waved it a fond farewell and watched it disappear over the horizon. The slight figure of Robert, glasses now steamed up, eased its way through the door with another crate of rum. He shouted over to us, 'Paolo! More ice on the way!'

All sorts of little scenarios were developing amongst the melee. In the corner by the bed, Linda was homing in on Giovanni, trying her best to get into his boiler suit. Three other Italian electricians danced on the table, spilling their drinks everywhere. The Shoppies seemed to be embroiled in some bizarre version of Twister, piled up in a big scrum in the middle of the room. The cabin was so full, you could not see the floor, but somehow bodies still came piling in through the door.

Zara elbowed me in the ribs. 'Looks like the ice has arrived!'

In through the door came two Italians in standard-issue grubby blue boiler suits open to the waist, arms aloft, carrying a tray of coffin-like proportions. Unable to manoeuvre the huge load past the heaving mass of sweaty bodies, they decided to simply dump it over the crowd and send a magnificent ice shower spraying across the room, much to everyone's delight. Indeed, so enamoured were they with the joy this evoked that they made three more ice runs, each climaxing in a triumphant ice-shower finale. A call to lifeboat stations at this point would not have come as a surprise, my cabin having taken on the appearance of the *Titanic* ballroom shortly after impact with the iceberg.

'Time to bail out.' Zara winked and led me out the door.

I awoke suddenly and looked at the clock on the bedside table.

'Shit.'

It was nine o'clock. I felt like crap and probably looked worse, and I was an hour late for clinic.

'Got to get to work,' I murmured to Zara, who was lying next to me, still fully clothed and half asleep.

'See you later,' she groaned.

I stumbled in the general direction of my room, half hoping I wouldn't be able to find it, anticipating the kind of state it would be in. The door was only slightly ajar, but I could already detect the tell-tale stench of stale beer and cigarettes. I went in, peering through half-opened bleary eyes. The first squelch was not a good sign. The second and third confirmed my worst fears; the carpet was completely sodden, wall to wall, and a few cigarette butts floated around in small pools of water like stranded lifeboats. Two people I had never seen before were strewn across the bare mattress of my bed, comatose, while all the sheets lay in a soggy pile under the table. On the table lay a spread-eagled boiler suit containing the last remnants of a wasted electrician. Beer cans, cigarette butts, and empty bottles were scattered widely around the room, even in the most unlikely of places, such as the wardrobe. And worst of all, a fire extinguisher, presumably empty, lay on the floor next to the waste bin.

This would mean trouble.

Although I arrived in the infirmary over an hour late, Linda, bless her, had held the fort during my absence, despite her own monumental hangover. Fortunately, the clinic had been quiet, but news of the party had already spread.

'The captain has called three times already, Paolo. I've tried to stall him, but he's not stupid, you know.'

No such luck, I thought. I called the bridge, fearing the worst.

Gambino answered. *'Doctor, can you come up to my office? I need to talk with you.'*

'Right now?'

'Yes. Right now.' And he hung up.

On the way up to the bridge, I tried to come up with some kind of excuse or explanation, but my brain was feeling too scrambled. The master gestured for me to sit down.

'Doctor. What happened last night? I am hearing all sorts of stories—wild parties, so much noise. The chief steward tells me your cabin is so much damaged. Tell me. What is going on?'

'It was my birthday,' came my pathetic reply. What did I expect, a present and a big kiss?

'Hmm. I don't know how you can let this happen. It's unbelievable,' he continued, making the most of this opportunity to twist the knife. 'You understand that as this has been reported to me by the chief steward and the chief of security, I must make a record in the ship's log.'

I envisioned his entry:

> Captain's Log, Star Date 233.4. After a brief skirmish with a Klingon battlecruiser in Sector Three, the *Lucky Star* moved into geostationary orbit around the planet Robbongi. Strangely, the doctor's quarters have been taken over by a destructive alien force, leaving three crew members dead. They all wore red boiler suits. Spock believes there may be a demonic spirit trying to take over the vessel through mind control. It seems that the doctor may now be under its hypnotic spell ...

'I understand ... I'm sorry. It won't happen again,' I replied flatly in my zomboid state.

The message was clear. The report would reach the Carnival office, and any further misdemeanour would land me in serious trouble. It transpired that all others present at the orgy of destruction were each issued with a written warning. Three of these would mean instant dismissal and a flight home.

A low profile would definitely be in order over the next few weeks. The legendary words of Clint Eastwood's *Dirty Harry* came to mind: 'A man's *got* to know his limitations.'

Exactly two weeks later, I found myself in the master's office again. This time, he was positively fuming, but I couldn't think why. He handed me a note and asked me to read it.

It said: *Passenger Comments, cruise no. LS#29.8.92. I was in a public establishment in Cozumel, and the doctor poured a beer over my head. I find this behaviour disrespectful, unprofessional, and he does not represent Carnival Cruise Lines.*

Busted again.

'Is this true?' Gambino asked, incredulously. His eyes were jumping from their sockets, and his lips quivered as his words passed over them.

'It's obviously an exaggeration. We were in Carlos 'N Charlies; you know what it's like in there. People were dancing around and spilling beer everywhere. I must have accidentally spilled some on her; I didn't even notice, to be honest,' I lied.

The fact of the matter was that I had deliberately emptied a beer bottle on her head. Why, I couldn't clearly recall. Not surprisingly, Gambino didn't believe my story, and the fact remained that the complaint was there in black and white.

'This is no good, Doctor,' ranted the captain. 'I will have to speak with Doctor Mo. Now go.'

This was it, I thought. *I've gone too far this time.* I could imagine Clint rolling his eyes in exasperation.

The passenger's comment would have come via the main office, so Mo must have already caught wind of the situation. I figured the only hope of saving my skin would be to speak to Mo myself as soon as possible. I walked down to the pier and found a pay phone.

'I presume you've read this complaint,' I ventured.

'What complaint?' came Mo's puzzled reply.

I explained the situation and decided to go for broke in the hope that Mo would take the complaint as a slur on his entire department, bringing into question his own credibility as medical director, for which he would fight hard.

'I don't want to cause all this trouble for you, and I can't expect you to take shit for this. I have decided to offer my resignation.'

Mo was stunned. *'No, Paolo. I won't let you. You are my one of my best doctors. No. Leave it with me. I'll sort this out.'*

'But…'

'Paolo,' Mo continued, 'leave it to me. Just don't get into any more trouble, okay?'

'Okay,' I replied meekly, satisfied that Mo's faith held firm. What a guy.

10

ALABAMA SLAMMER

August and early September had been a dangerous period. Gambino hung a catalogue of misdemeanours over my head like the Sword of Damocles, and he couldn't wait to use it to slice me up. He had weaponised the blossoming romance between nurse Barbie and David Gardner, the powerful hotel manager of the Limp Moustache, to infiltrate the heart of my infirmary. I had been oblivious to the spies in our midst, and Gambino had the upper hand. I was fully aware that I was still under siege.

But satisfied that I'd fulfilled my professional duties without blemish, my powerful ally Dr Mo had fended off Gambino's attack on my Caribbean adventure. And I took heart that my repeated indiscipline had occurred outside the clinical realm. Barbie and David's recent transfer to another ship proved another win. Knowing that Gambino lay in wait, I vowed to shift my focus back to my department and professional life.

By this time, Barbie's replacement had been onboard for four weeks. Hailing from Mississippi, her southern drawl was very Barbie-like, but that's where any similarity abruptly ended. In stark contrast to Barbie's petite, doll-like appearance, Betty had the physique of the ancient stone statue of the Venus of Willendorf: all breasts, bottom, and thighs. The undulating rolls of flab cascading down every inch of her five-foot frame filled her uniform to capacity and threatened to burst at every seam. But Betty was quite a character; fun and easygoing with a raucous sense of humour, and her favourite work-related catchphrase soon caught on with rest of the medical team: *CYA—Cover Your Ass!*

It was clear that Betty had been around the block a few times over the course of her forty-odd years, and the combination of her extreme physique and boisterous personality made her quite endearing to us. She was our very own pocket battleship.

When Betty first arrived onboard, there was some vague problem with her allocated cabin, so she had to move into a small makeshift side-room in the infirmary that was transformed into her new sleeping quarters. Surprisingly, she accepted this move without any fuss and seemed quite happy to be living within the department.

It was left to Linda and Valeria to remark on the increasingly steady stream of out-of-hours infirmary visits by crew members of a particular type since Betty's arrival. Some mornings, we'd arrive to start the daily clinic, only to encounter a Jamaican cabin steward or a Haitian galley-hand skulking about the infirmary in an obviously failed attempt at escaping unnoticed. On several other occasions when Linda or Valeria had been called to attend the infirmary in the evening, Betty would suddenly appear from her quarters looking rather flustered and hot-under-the-collar. Later, when the out-of-hours patient had left, one of Betty's Boys would sidle out from her room and make for a sheepish exit. It seemed the boys below deck found her exaggerated, voluptuous form irresistible, and each night they would regularly pay homage to the ancient Goddess of Fertility.

The number of visitors escalated with each passing week, leading us to believe there might be more to it than just Betty's fancy. We never knew whether her makeshift maritime fertility fetish museum charged an entrance fee.

Had Sweaty Betty initiated her own small business venture since coming aboard? Was the infirmary side-room now a salacious boudoir hosting a select-crew prostitution racket?

I wondered how to address this issue. If we were wrong, that would be a major embarrassment. Besides, we liked Betty. Maybe she was simply like the rest of us, out to have the most fun onboard that she possibly could? I took time to consider my options.

If I was going to reveal my suspicions to anybody, it would be to Dr Mo, and him alone. And certainly not Gambino, who would unquestionably see whoring and debauchery in the medical department as ammunition to help strike me down. Fortunately, I knew the captain's attention was fully focused on the ship's upcoming biennial maintenance programme, which would see it taken out of passenger service to be refurbished and repaired at the dry dock in Mobile, Alabama.

During this time, many of the ship's internal systems would be shut down, which afforded non-essential officers some shore leave. Medical staff were included in this. The *Lucky Star* was technically on US soil during this period, and I was only registered to work as a doctor while at sea. The local Mobile ambulance service would have to deal with any medical emergency amongst those who remained onboard.

As the *Lucky Star* departed Miami for the last passenger-heavy cruise before dry dock, a few of us got together and looked into planning our time off in Mobile. None of us had been to Alabama before, so apart from a game of golf and maybe visiting some local restaurants, we were rather short on ideas.

The other great unknown was exactly how long our shore leave would last. The docking facility charged Carnival by the hour, so the company made every effort to work quickly and minimise the expense. It could be anywhere between two and six days. The only certainty was that New Orleans was only a two-hour drive away. Opportunity beckoned.

Rob pointed out another interesting idea: in the next seven days, we all had the chance to meet a girl from Alabama. This could add some spice to an otherwise potentially boring week in dry dock. The challenge was set.

I looked up at the huge map of the United States stuck on my cabin wall. I'd bought it soon after joining the *Lucky Star* with the intention of planning a big US road trip once my stint with *Carnival* was over. But a different kind of cartographical challenge presented itself after a night of passion with a cone from Myrtle Beach, South Carolina. She insisted on marking her home town with a big X on the map. Six months down the track, the map had become dotted with an array of large Xs in red marker pen, documenting my Coning Tour of the US while at sea. And as it turned out, there was one glaringly obvious omission amongst the more heavily peppered Dixieland zone: the state of Alabama.

As luck would have it, the gods were smiling that week. Her name was Sherri, and she was from Montgomery, Alabama. This lively young lady was celebrating her twenty-fourth birthday onboard with a group of friends, and as we took a shine to each other, I was invited to join in with her celebrations. By the end of her cruise, we made plans to catch up again in Mobile the following week. And Rob owed me a beer.

Once our last group of passengers had disembarked, the *Lucky Star* sailed overnight from Miami around the southern tip of Florida and into the Gulf of Mexico, from which point we headed north. By morning, we had reached Mobile Bay. In our sights dead ahead appeared the formidable visage of the WWII battleship USS *Alabama*, docked permanently at the end of a small headland. Our ship turned to port and entered the Mobile River, sailing slowly past the huge shipyard structures and container terminals along the shoreline before reaching our very own docking facility.

Our vessel carefully manoeuvred into the vast enclosure, and the massive steel gates shut behind us. Watching the water level slowly diminish from under the ship was a sight to behold, and several hours later, the enclosed dock was indeed dry. The 46,000-tonne *Lucky Star* was now held aloft by massive concrete and steel supports. Fascinated by this process, Linda and I went for a walk down under the ship, cameras in hand, to view the barnacle-riddled hull and the ship's two massive twenty-foot bronze propellers, which were now clearly visible. The dock was bustling with dozens of shipyard workers and machinery, ready to begin the intense cleaning and repair process.

Our interest in this unique event didn't last long. Soon enough, the ship's air-conditioning was switched off. Then the indoor lighting. And shortly afterwards, the onboard sewerage system ground to a halt. Life onboard ship would now require a flashlight, an electric fan, a bucket of water to purge the toilets, and a peg for your nose. The next twenty-four hours proved to be a difficult and disgusting period, with the hot and humid Alabama climate contributing to the sticky and smelly situation.

The next day, it was clear what had to be done. The nurses found a nearby motel and decamped for the next few days. I decided to foot the bill for their lodging fees myself, as the nurses' pay rate wasn't great compared to my own. I figured it was the decent thing to do, given the nasty environment onboard ship. As for myself, I arranged to meet Sherri at the downtown Holiday Inn.

I went up to the bridge to inform the captain of my plans.

'That's fine, Doctor,' replied Gambino.

'If you need me for anything, I'll be staying at the Holiday Inn. Do you know when we'll be leaving dry dock yet?'

'No. We'll decide when it looks like the work is nearly done. It'll probably take about four or five days.'

'Okay. So how do I find out when we're going to leave? Is there a phone here I can call?'

This was getting a bit sticky.

Gambino scribbled down a phone number on a scrap of paper.

'Here. This is Bob Norris's office number,' he abruptly informed me. 'He's the ship's agent in Mobile.'

I stuffed the note into my pocket and left the bridge, focusing on the appealing thought of getting off that hot and sweaty ship and into the arms of my hot and steamy Alabama gal.

We spent that night at the Mobile Holiday Inn and dined out at Ruth's Chris Steak House, the best ribeye I've ever had. But New Orleans was a-calling, with its rich cultural history, renowned musical tradition, and delicious Louisiana cuisine, not to mention its reputation as party town extraordinaire. It might offer the perfect respite for a ship-weary officer, I thought, complete with my own sassy tour guide to boot.

We sped along the southern coast of Mississippi, and I mused about one of my favourite movies. Starring Mickey Rourke and Robert De Niro, *Angel Heart* is set in 1950s New Orleans. This dark and fearsome psychological thriller takes Rourke's character, the private detective Harry Angel, deep into the mysterious local underworld, where he encounters a series of disturbing and horrific events heavily connected to the practice of voodoo and black magic. It is a brilliant film but also an unnerving introduction to the world-famous city of the Deep South.

Sherri and I arrived on the much-vaunted Bourbon Street and checked in to a hotel at two o'clock in the afternoon. The street, famous for hosting the annual Mardi Gras, still had that epochal 19th-century feel. Tightly packed two- and three-storied townhouses with intricate facades, overhanging balconies, and decorative wrought-iron railings lined the narrow, pedestrianised route.

We took our time strolling along the famous locale, stopping at the many bars and live jazz venues dotted along the way. Most of these spots were very inviting, while others housed ramshackle strip joints and scruffy dives that heralded the street's sleazier reputation. Sherri introduced me to the Screaming Nazi, a searing combo shot of Jägermeister and Rumple Minze peppermint schnapps, which hits you like a blitzkrieg assault from a Wehrmacht Panzer division. And then there was the Hurricane, New Orleans' gold-standard beverage that fuelled the rest of our afternoon.

It seemed like every few yards, we would come across a Hurricane shop. They all displayed a short row of what looked like small washing machines, each churning a different coloured mix, forming a dazzling rainbow of choices from red, orange, and yellow through to the blues and purples. Different fruit flavours were combined with a selection of light and dark rums, topped with an undisclosed quantity of overproof rum, and served up in a huge plastic cup. The mere thought of overproof rum gave me flashbacks to the deadly concoctions served up by Dave at Picadilly's in Nassau, but my inner dread had to take a back seat. When in Rome …

A few hours later, I was struggling to keep up. Sherri had the constitution of an ox and was happily taking on the Hurricanes like a Greek goddess, impervious to the high-velocity Aegean winds. It may have been a harbinger of my developing stupor, but in one live bar we stopped at, I was convinced we had witnessed the reincarnated Jimi Hendrix. A young, slim black guitarist kitted out in psychedelic 60s gear mesmerised us with his extraordinary skills playing number after number from the rock legend's fabled repertoire. And I swear he was left-handed.

By now, the colourful Hurricanes had led me into my own purple haze, and just around the corner, we stumbled upon the New Orleans Voodoo Museum. The beaten old wooden door led into a tiny reception area, beyond which we could see into the museum itself: a small, dimly lit room bedecked with paintings of ritual ceremonies, scary wooden masks, and an array of Catholic-looking artefacts perched upon a small altar. Over on the side was a rather disturbing collection of human skulls set on spikes and a few woven voodoo dolls stuck onto the peeling wall.

'Shit. That looks a bit scary,' I suggested.

'Yeah, that voodoo stuff is spooky,' agreed Sherri, peering into the dark enclave. 'D'ya wanna go in?'

'Hmm, not sure,' I replied.

Suddenly, a dark, wizened old man popped up from nowhere into the space behind the front desk.

'Welcome to the Voodoo Museum,' he announced in a slow and deliberate tone. 'Would you folks like a psychic reading?'

The man's dramatic appearance and theatrical delivery caught me off balance.

'Um … maybe.'

A well-worn melon-sized 'crystal' ball resting on a brass stand stood on the counter. The painted sign read *Resident Voodoo Practitioner: Bobby Moore.*

I cracked into a half-smile. 'So … your name is Bobby Moore?'

His dour countenance was unmoved. 'Yes. That is correct. I can give you a psychic reading for ten dollars.'

But I couldn't contain myself and I cracked up, laughing uncontrollably.

Sherri grabbed my arm sternly. 'What's so funny?'

'His name …' I was only able to let out a few staccatoed words between cackles. 'Bobby … hahahahaha … Moore … hahahahaha!'

The disgruntled Mr Moore started to raise his voice. 'And what is wrong with that?'

'Sorry, I can't help it,' I tried to explain in between fits of giggles. 'Bobby Moore is …'

But then Sherri grabbed my arm and marched us both towards the exit.

'Sorry, Mr Moore,' she apologised, dragging me out. 'He's pretty smashed.'

'Get out!' Mr Voodoo yelled back; his eyes now wide with rage as he pointed to the door. 'We don't need your kind in here!'

Once outside, I managed to explain to Sherri what had got me going. Bobby Moore was a stratospherically famous

English football player, captain of England's legendary 1966 World Cup winning team. Blonde, blue-eyed, and with a calm and stoic nature, Bobby was the complete antithesis of his New Orleans Voodoo namesake

'Jesus!' Sherri scolded me. 'That was so embarrassing.'

'I know. I'm sorry, I just couldn't help it.'

'Let's get out of here before he casts a spell on you or something.'

Perhaps Jimi's Voodoo Child was a-stirring.

Turning back onto Bourbon, I heard someone yell out my name from across the street.

'Hey, Paolo!' It was Valeria from the ship.

'Hi, Valeria. How you going?'

'Yeah, I'm fine. But listen, I'm heading back to Mobile tonight. I've heard the ship might be leaving tomorrow.'

'Really?' I replied, trying to rectify my staggering gait.

'Yeah. I don't know for sure, but that's the word on the street. Don't stay out too late!'

Valeria took off, leaving me in a heightened state of confusion. What was I to do? I fumbled around in my pocket for that number Gambino had given me, and I managed to find a pay phone nearby. I called the agent's office. But it was now after hours, and there was no answer.

I put my drunken self into Gambino's shoes. With so many crew scattered across Alabama and beyond, an early dawn departure seemed unlikely. Plus, international maritime law meant that he would have to wait for the ship's doctor before setting sail. It was a little risky, but it would have to wait till morning; Sherri and I were far too drunk to drive back now.

Our night out could have taken a nosedive there and then, but what the heck, we were enjoying the Big Easy, and an early night wasn't on the agenda. We found a quiet spot and chilled out for a while.

At the bar, we got talking to the wealthy and sophisticated Jerry and Denise, both New Orleans locals. They were very good company and were intrigued by our story, which had led us to Bourbon Street. After a few more drinks, they invited us to their favourite local restaurant for dinner, where they'd already booked a table. It seems you really can't beat good ol' southern hospitality.

The Bon Ton Cafe served old-school classic Louisiana cuisine, and the wooden panelling and red-and-white checked tablecloths enhanced the traditional atmosphere inside. We had a great time sampling the crawfish étouffée and other fantastic local delights. And if that wasn't enough, our new-found friends invited us back to their swanky apartment just off Bourbon Street for a nightcap. A nightcap indeed. A few more hours of chat and laughter took us deep into the night.

Maybe it was the thought of our early morning run to Mobile that made me edgy. But this situation was starting to make me paranoid. In the UK, finding yourself at the home of two complete strangers who'd shouted you dinner after randomly meeting them in bar was outlandishly and weirdly friendly. It just didn't happen. Maybe it was just that stiff, ultra-reserved area of my British brain that had taken control, the Big Uneasy.

But were Jerry and Denise genuine? Maybe they had lured a couple of drunken strays into their dark web where a horrific denouement loomed just around the corner. Perhaps they were good mates of the all-powerful Mr Voodoo?

What would Harry Angel have done?

The next morning, we awoke from our slumber a bit later than we'd hoped. It was eight o'clock. The journey back to Mobile would take two hours on the I-10 freeway, so we grabbed a quick breakfast, packed our bags, and headed for the ship I had left only two days earlier.

We arrived at the Mobile dry dock only to find … absolutely nothing.

'What … the …' I stuttered.

'What's going on?' Sherri was just as perplexed.

'The bloody ship's gone!' I couldn't believe it. What the hell was happening?

'Are you sure this is the right place?'

'Hang on. Let's have a look around.'

Sherri and I drove around the nearby docks, desperately searching for a whole 46,000-tonne cruise ship that had disappeared without trace. But alas, it was to no avail. Without further delay, we made a dash to the Holiday Inn, where reception handed me a message: *Call Bob Norris 9867-7876.*

I quickly called Bob, who informed me that the *Lucky Star* had sailed off just thirty minutes earlier. At least Mr Norris was in possession of all my belongings, which had been quickly packed up and unceremoniously dumped on the pier, as per Captain's orders.

Gambino had finally done it.

Our long-running feud was over, and I had well and truly lost The Game.

11
BACK TO BASICS

Feeling refreshed and recharged after a brief unscheduled vacation, I arrived in Nassau to take up duty once again on the tss *Carnivale*. Still smarting from the embarrassing episode in Mobile, I was happy to be relegated to the forgotten backwaters of the Carnival fleet. My action-packed seven months on the *Lucky Star* had been a real-life cross between *The Love Boat* and *Carry On Cruising*: fun and challenging, but also very stressful at times.

I was glad to hear that Dirk was still on the *Mardi Gras*, so we arranged to meet up at Piccadilly's for a few drinks. I was warmly greeted by the ever-smiling Dave.

'Hey, Doc! Long time no see. How's it going?' He grinned as we firmly shook hands.

'Fine.' I winced.

Dirk was happy to see me but obviously had something on his mind. Knowing his forthright manner, it came as no surprise when the obvious question was put on the table.

'So, I heard you missed the ship. What happened?'

'Well, it's a long story. Basically, I was on a bender in New Orleans with a girl from Alabama. But by the time we got back to Mobile the next day, the ship had gone.'

'Jesus! I hope she was worth it. But how come you're still here—you didn't get fired?'

Dave proceeded to pour us both a special shooter, welcoming my return to Nassau. Suffice to say, the measure of 151 alone could have propelled Apollo 11 to the moon and back.

'Well, of course I called Mo afterwards. I was expecting it to be the last time I would ever speak to him.'

'So, what did he say?'

'Well, that's the funny thing. Mo was great! Even though I missed the ship, he still backed me up and was happy for me to continue with Carnival. So here I am!'

We laughed heartily and toasted the magnificent Dr Mo before sculling our extra-high-octane cocaine shooters.

I was so grateful that Dr Mo had faith in my doctoring skills and still backed me up despite my catalogue of misdemeanours.

'Good old Mo; he really is our guardian angel!'

I was still thinking about the ongoing battle I had with the master of the *Lucky Star*. I revealed to Dirk what was still on my mind.

'I do have a suspicion that Captain Gambino might have planned the whole thing. I don't know for sure; it's just a guess. Did you get that letter I sent you, explaining the feud I had with him?'

'Yeah, I did, so maybe he did try to get rid of you? Who knows?'

We raised our deadly shooters in celebration that I was still around.

'Here's to Captain Gambino!' I exclaimed in my drunken state.

Dirk joined in with another joke about the master. 'Yeah. And good job it didn't involve a concrete overcoat and a swim in the Mobile River!'

I had also gained some interesting information about what happened after I missed the ship.

'I spoke to Linda, the nurse on the *Lucky Star*, yesterday. She told me all about the doctor who replaced me in Mobile.'

'So, what happened?'

'Well, Linda told me that Mo managed to get a doctor from the local hospital in Mobile. He came aboard, and Linda didn't know what his expectations were, but work was not one of them! Apparently, he was out of his depth and could not in four days find his own way to the infirmary, his cabin, or the dining room. He drank copiously; all the booze stored in Betty's cabin and the infirmary was all gone. The nurses had to collect him and propel him around everywhere. He was incensed to find that he was not dining at the captain's table nor mixing in elevated circles. When they reached Miami, he had already put many calls in to Carnival demanding many ridiculous requests, including exorbitant wages and reimbursements and a private helicopter back to New Orleans.'

Dirk's jaw dropped to the ground.

'Wow, that doctor sounds crazy. After those four days, maybe Gambino wanted you back! Haha!'

'Ha! That would be hilarious!'

Ten minutes later, I felt a little more drunk.

Twenty minutes later, I felt like I should have a little lie down; after all, it was still only six o'clock.

Three hours later, I woke up in my cabin, feeling a bit fuzzy but ready for action. But that's about as far as I got; my legs had turned to rubber, and I couldn't stand up.

I felt like I had been transported back in time to one of our medical school wine-tasting evenings hosted by the professor of microbiology, a jovial wine connoisseur. He used to get around on two prosthetic legs as a result of a severe injury many years previously. Of course, the recurring joke was that by the end of the evening, we would *all* become legless.

I flailed away vainly on my cabin floor like a dying fly at an ice rink: zero for technical merit, but a glorious ten for artistic impression. As if this wasn't enough, attempting to speak simply resulted in my lips wobbling up and down in a shower of spit. I was well and truly blasted and resigned myself to crashing out after only one drink.

I hope the Boys don't get to hear of this.

So now I was back on the old *Carnivale*, I would have more time on my hands, and I could concentrate on more weighty matters like becoming an expert card player. I had long been interested in poker, ever since being taught to play five-card draw at the kitchen table by my grandpa, who introduced me to Stonewall Jackson by bluffing me out of my pocket money. But in Britain, poker was not widely played as it is in the US, so my ambition to become world poker champion had been shelved indefinitely from the age of twelve. Then one glorious day, during an interminably long wait at Miami airport, I happened to pick up a copy of Anthony Holden's new book, *Big Deal: One Year as a Professional Poker Player*. I was inspired!

Making the leap from experienced amateur playing a regular Tuesday night game, Holden takes the plunge and decides to join the pro circuit, playing in tournaments all around the world, culminating in the World Series of Poker at Binion's Horseshoe Casino in Las Vegas. Already a well-known and respected writer, Holden brilliantly described all the aspects of the game, which I found so enthralling: the psychological cut and thrust of poker play, the camaraderie found on the professional circuit, and some of the more colourful characters involved at the game's highest level, like the great Texan, Amarillo 'Slim' Preston.

But getting a game going on the ship was to prove difficult, as no-one was really interested. All except for Alex, that is, a new recruit from England. He held the official title of sanitation officer, which, he was eager to explain, wasn't anything to do with toilets.

'I kill cockroaches,' he chirped. 'Used to work for Rentokil in London. You name it, we killed it: cockroaches, rats, mice, wasps!'

He took his hand from the pocket of his dirty, off-white boiler suit and made a shooting gesture with his thumb and forefinger. 'Pigeons too. Filthy vermin,' he said, taking aim.

'So, what are you doing here?' I asked.

'Cockroaches. There are millions of the bastards here. You should go down to the galley; the place is crawling with 'em.'

'Really?'

'Yeah, you should see them; it's disgusting. I've been spraying them for a week solid now, but they just keep coming back for more. I'll take you down there to have a look if you like.'

'Hmm. So, you won't be able to fix my toilet then?' I ventured.

Seven months away from the steaming *Carnivale,* and nothing much had changed. On my return, I was warmly greeted by the rancid eructations of that burbling-bottom burper of a lavatory in the doctor's cabin.

Alex scratched his recently cropped head in hesitation, but his good nature and eagerness to please got the better of him.

'Well, I could have a look at it for you…'

It was too late for protestations; as far as I was concerned, the new ship's sanitation officer was going to attend to some urgent onboard sanitary business.

Two hours, one plunger, a set of heavy spanners, and one bottle of rum later, Alex and I had just about managed to flood my room with the feculent contents of the ship's bilge pump. Since the beginning of recorded history, this toilet had spat out filth in a rather intermittent and polite manner, but somehow, we had managed to transform it into some kind of wrathful spiritual presence, a monstrous ceramic pagan god spewing forth its molten lava in vengeance on its mortal subjects. The whole damn cabin was covered in shit, and we were caked in the stuff. But good old Ron Bacardi had seen to it that we were still in good spirits.

Not to worry, we thought. *Shit happens.*

Our time spent sailing the high seas was not quite the never-ending adventure it sometimes appeared. There were times when extreme boredom set in. Quiet days at sea, confined to the same old boat with the same old faces and same old food. After a few months, even Mr Kim's seemingly endless supply of porno videos started to wear a bit thin. Alex and I probably had the cushiest numbers on the ship, and as a result were often at a loose end. Sunbathing could only be tolerated for so long, especially for Alex, whose fair complexion, born, unlike Lee Marvin, under a wandering Manchester cloud, would turn lobster-esque at the mere sight of a sunbeam. We could read books, but we never had much chance to buy any decent ones (personally, I can't recommend a good bookshop in Nassau). And once we had seen every show, dance, comedian, or musician onboard for the fiftieth time, that blustery 'Oklahoma' medley and hackneyed ventriloquist act kind of lost their appeal. And bingo was totally out of the question—death by a thousand cuts being a more inviting prospect.

One day, we got so utterly bored that we created an entire game based on ship-board life, complete with Monopoly-like board, counters, and action cards. The main objective of the game was to retrieve the oversized undergarments of the friendly, ruddy-faced Glaswegian Carnival vice-president of operations (pair of 44-inch Y-fronts included) from a certain location on the ship. Then, proudly wearing the Y-fronts on your head when rolling the dice, skilfully escape from the ship while trying to avoid incurring penalties or written warnings along the way. Other players could chase you around the decks and try to win the Y-fronts off you, making their own escape possible. In effect, a subtle, sophisticated strategy game of skill and high drama for all ages. Watch out for Brendan Corrigan's Underpants (BCU)™ in the shops next Christmas—it's going to be a massive hit.

But even though BCU was an instant smash, the famed Scottish jocks were eventually consigned to the scrap heap after a short stint in the limelight. Other inventions to relieve the boredom included fruit baseball: one aluminium-tungsten alloy Louisville Slugger baseball bat; a selection of cantaloupes, pumpkins, and watermelons; and a large grassy field in Port Canaveral. You can imagine the result: very messy but great therapy.

But in the end, it was a deck of cards that saved our brains from the combined numbing effect of repeated hangovers and hour upon hour of tediously blue skies. Ah, yes, life was tough.

And so it was that Alex and I endeavoured to break the monotony by becoming champion card players. Inspired by the enthralling exploits of 'English Tony', as the Americans tagged our hero in *Big Deal*, Alex and I began to learn the intricacies of Texas hold 'em, seven-card stud, and other poker variations. Plus, blackjack. We managed to get our hands on some more books on card playing, and we were able to refine our skills while enjoying a few 'friendly' games with anyone who we could muster, be it animal, vegetable, mineral, or Italian. But after a few months of this, we realised that we needed to spread our wings and take on a wider challenge. Poker was by far the more interesting to play, but decent games were hard to come by. After digesting the standard texts and consulting the recognised gurus on the subject, our next mission became clear—to take on the casinos of the Bahamas.

Three times a week, our ship docked in ports equipped with a hotel and casino, and here we could practice our skills on the blackjack tables and take the world by storm.

When most people think of blackjack, they usually split into two camps. One, the blind optimist group, believe that winning or losing depends entirely on luck and the random fall of the cards. These people will have some fun playing, but most likely will come out losers. The second group are the punters who understand the basic strategy of blackjack and follow the statistical rules to maximise their chances. But even a perfect by-the-book technique gives up a 1.5% advantage to the house. In the long run, this small difference will wear them down, and over time, these too will lose. Only, they won't enjoy it.

But there is a third way: card-counting.

By becoming skilled in memorising cards and recognising patterns of play, in combination with the basic strategy, card-counting can give the player a small but vital edge over the house. And the casinos don't like that one bit. They call it cheating. It takes a great deal of practice, concentration, and mental agility to bring it off, and in my opinion, it's simply playing the game to the best of one's ability but still within the rules. But it's their table, and they'll cry if they want to.

As its name suggests, card-counting involves keeping a mental track of the cards that have already been in play, and in its most basic form, noting the balance between high (ten, J, Q, K) and low (two to six) value cards. The running count gives the rough probability of the next card being a ten value. Statistically, high cards are good for the player and bad for the house, so a count that strongly suggests plenty of tens left in the pack will spur the counter to bet heavily, expecting a winning hand. But even though card-counting involves no underhand practice, signals, equipment, or gadgetry, it is deemed 'illegal' by nearly every casino on the planet for the simple reason that it works. Mention this unholy practice to a casino boss, and he'll go into a fit of acute apoplexy before having you removed from the premises by several large men in tight-fitting tuxedos.

This totally unreasonable dogma has led to the farcical scenario in which professional gamblers have taken to donning false beards and even more sophisticated disguises in order to earn their living at the blackjack tables. Pit bosses are on their guard for these characters, and they can also be alerted by a card-counter's characteristic betting pattern; they bet quietly until the count is favourable, then come in suddenly with a large bet. So, part of the acquired skill is to disguise this recognisable pattern from the suspicious gaze of the bosses without it affecting your strategy.

In addition to the strong-arm tactics, casinos also adopt a more subtle approach to deter the counters. Keeping track of the cards in a single fifty-two card deck is relatively easy, so the casino will use four, six, or even eight decks in the shoe. To find a casino that uses just one or two decks is the card-counters idea of nirvana. The count's predictive powers become far more accurate near to the end of the deck when fewer cards remain, so the dastardly house uses that annoying little plastic card to cut the pack for the next shuffle, a long way before the end of the shoe is reached.

So that's about four balls that the card-counter has to juggle in the air at the same time, all while trying to maintain an air of calmness and composure.

After some initial reconnaissance missions to the three casinos, including some practice under live conditions with small cash amounts, we formulated our plan and decided to take on the Paradise Island Casino.

This was going to be *it*.

The Sting.

The Big Tuna.

Maybe even the *Giant Mackerel*.

12

MEN OF MYSTERY

At eight o'clock sharp, the Dudes appeared at the top of the gangplank, the early March sun having long since departed. Pausing for effect, we acknowledged the stares of disbelief from embarking passengers as they admired our carefully crafted get-up. The outstandingly loud nature of our colourful suits was equalled only by their sheer lack of quality. For me, crotch-numbingly tight orange-and-red-striped stretch-polyester bell-bottom pants, combined with a badly fitting red, white, and blue checked jacket in the nastiest polyester money can buy. The sartorial disaster was topped off by a black ruffled shirt with fuck-off collars and a set of impenetrable black sunglasses. Alex sported the same hideous trousers in a radioactive turquoise-and-pink hue with an oversized powder-blue sports jacket over a shirt-and-tie combination worthy of a colour-blind surrealist. A set of saucer-like brown plastic shades completed his nasty ensemble.

It's amazing what you can pick up in the quality boutiques around Nassau.

Just to embellish the sleazy tone, my thick, dark hair was now matted to my scalp with a disgustingly liberal application of Brylcreem. The pièce de résistance, however, had to be the beard. Lovingly cultivated into a lush thicket over the preceding four weeks and then attacked by Alex with a barber's razor, I was now the proud owner of a menacing biker's moustache and a set of outrageous porkchop sideburns. This was topped off by a stick-on neck tattoo depicting a flying eagle with a banner reading *Live to Ride*.

We made our way down to the pier with a nod here and a wave there as bewildered tourists stumbled up the steps. Even crew members and close friends looked puzzled as they sidled past, keen not to get too close. It soon dawned on us that nobody at all recognised us as the friendly neighbourhood ship's doctor and sanitation officer.

At first, it was a strange feeling, but also rather empowering. The sudden realisation that we were free to compose two wholly new and previously unknown characters filled our veins with a powerful and invigorating appetite for adventure. Neither of us knew quite who we were supposed to be or what exactly was going to happen, but for the moment, we would simply bask in the freedom of anonymity and head off into the unknown.

Right on cue, a taxi pulled up on the pier, and appropriately enough, it was not the usual clapped-out old bomb often seen trundling around Nassau. No, this was a gleaming, sleek white Mercedes stretch limousine, and as the sparkling wheels came to a smooth halt on the tarmac, the back door magically opened and beckoned us inside.

But I hesitated before getting in.

In truth, I was a little nervous about the blackjack. We had each stumped up half the bankroll, and this small roll of hundred-dollar bills just large enough to cause a visible bulge (though not quite salami-sized) in my admittedly tight pants was about to make its long-awaited debut. Strictly speaking, card-counting at blackjack is a long-term strategy where one can eke out a steady profit with discipline and persistence. But this was not our style, and we had decided to go for broke in one night of do-or-die action. It would be suicide for both of us to play, and I was to be the one in the hot seat. We had formed an unbreakable duo and pledged to ourselves to end the night as kings of the casino or to go down in a blaze of glory. And somewhere in between was simply not on the agenda. I knew that Alex had confidence in my skills, and he was happy to play the sidekick for the card game, but I did feel a little uneasy with the responsibility.

I looked over to Alex.

'This is it, mate,' he said, slapping me on the back. 'Whatever happens with the cards, let's just have a good night, eh?'

'Yeah. It *will* be a good night,' I replied. 'I can feel it in my water.'

Good old Alex. We had become an inseparable double act during the past four months, and it felt good to have found such a great friend in this soulless environment.

I began to feel more relaxed already, so I held the limo door open and waved Alex inside with a flamboyant swish of the arm.

'After you, my good man.'

'Thank you, dude.'

As we made ourselves comfortable in the back of the sumptuous automobile, Alex broke into that mischievous schoolboy smile that he had, as if about to go and do something naughty behind the bike sheds. Then he started to giggle uncontrollably.

'Just look at the fucking state of us!'

'I know, I know. Can you believe it? What a couple of twats!'

'I tell you what, Paolo, if we just survive the night in one piece, I'll be happy,' he laughed, lighting up his first cigarette of the night. 'Christ knows what the casino will make of us. We'll be lucky to even get in.'

'Ah, but tonight we are high rollers, and the world is our lobster! Show them no mercy and they won't know what hit them.'

'Right on, dude! Buy the ticket; take the ride!'

We laughed heartily at this prospect as the limousine sped us to our date with destiny.

The limo pulled up outside Paradise Island Casino, and Alex handed the grateful cabby a crisp fifty-dollar note, instructing him to keep the change. The casino was huge. From the front door, it was but a short step along the purple carpet to the gaming area, but as usual in these cathedrals of greed, it was first necessary to negotiate the many pews of clanking fruit machines—how those mindless monsters annoy me. All that irritating electronic clanging and banging, the mindless repetition of coin, pull, blank stare, coin, pull, blank stare of the slot junkies. It's hard to resist taking a sledgehammer to the lot. Once past this annoying din, the atmosphere changed for the better.

The brightly lit main room must have covered half a football pitch, with at least twenty blackjack tables arranged in a horseshoe at the near end. Further away, the yelps and screams unique to the craps tables could be heard over the more orderly background chatter emanating from the blackjack and baccarat crowds close by. Bang in the middle of all this, a huge, neon-lit wheel of fortune spun lazily, adorned by two bikini-clad dolly-birds draping themselves seductively over the main prize—a spanking new cherry-red Chevy pick-up truck. It was still early in the evening, and the tables were not too busy, as we had anticipated. But still there was a palpable excitement in the air. The punters here were happy—they were on holiday; it was still early, which meant they hadn't lost all their money yet; and, as is customary at such casinos, players were welcome to partake in free alcoholic drinks while at the tables.

'Let's get a few drinks,' Alex suggested while scanning the room.

'Good idea. Dressed like this, I'll need at least two rum and cokes in me before we do *anything*.'

'Look,' said Alex, pointing off to the right, 'there's a bar over there.'

'Roger that.'

It soon dawned that we were on show as people began to stare and point. A frisson of anticipation shivered its way down my spine, and I could feel my new persona take a greater hold with each step. Alex felt it too.

Over the course of the next forty paces, I saw Alex visibly metamorphosise from cheeky cockroach-killer into a swaggering high roller with a fistful of attitude. His expression transformed from jocular grin to murderous stare quicker than you could say 'concrete overcoat'. Each passing look was met with a steely gaze, painfully skewering the curious passers-by to the nearest pillar as he struck fear deep into their hearts. Alex had left himself behind and moved to another plane in the blink of an eye. It was an inspiring transformation, worthy of Dr Hunter S Thompson himself, yet so far free from intoxicants. Taking up the reins, I held my head high and sniffed the heady aroma of invincibility left in his wake. *So, this is what it's like to be noticed, to be almost famous,* I thought. And it was good.

'Hey guys, what can I get you?' asked the bemused young bartender as we approached.

'Well, now, let me see here,' I started, thinking of a suitable drinks order for a couple of likely geezers. And as the words came out, I became lost in the moment and began to speak *in tongues*. My subconscious had absorbed all the bizarre ingredients over the previous few hours and concluded that my resulting persona for the evening would be a South African sleazeball with a hint of Dr Mo thrown in.

So, I found myself conversing in dude-speak with a broad Afrikaaner accent—not the most harmonious of combinations, but I suppose that just added another element of surreality to the proceedings.

'Hey, my friend.' I added a Huggy Bear style hand gesture for good measure, pointing lazily at nothing. 'Make mine a tequila sunrise, *ja*.'

'And your friend?'

Alex was busy surveying the scene. He was in some kind of twilight zone, silent.

'My good friend will heve an Elebema slemmer, *ja*. Thenk you. Thenk you very much.'

The bartender smiled to himself and turned to mix the drinks.

A couple of convivial cocktails later, the Dudes were fuelled and ready for action. Alex was now in a place of his own and had fully taken on the role of menacing henchman. He led the way, sternly clearing a path to the blackjack tables, constantly scanning the room through his dark shades for potential assassination attempts. Occasionally, he threatened to reach into his inner jacket pocket with a nervous trigger finger, but each time, he resisted the temptation to blow the head off the oblivious tourist in his path.

I was freewheeling and letting the subconscious flow take over.

We spotted a fifty-dollar table (fifty-dollar minimum bet) with a few vacant seats, so we perched ourselves on a couple of stools. Obviously, we didn't have the cash to play with the *real* high rollers, but in our current crazy microcosm, we felt that anything was possible. The other punters looked on curiously as I unveiled our wad of hundred-dollar bills.

'Hey, ma man!' I hailed the croupier, delivering our bankroll with a flamboyant swish. 'Can ya kesh these notes in for some chips. Thenks.'

At first, the fresh-faced young man looked a bit dumbstruck by our arrival, but he pulled himself together and made for the cash box.

'Aye, of course sir,' he replied in a northern English accent and proceeded to count out my pile of chips.

'Thet's an English eccent you have there, *ja*?'

'That's right. I'm from Manchester.'

'Ah, very interesting. Getting a bit more sun over here in the Bahamas then!'

'Yeah, although I don't get a lot of time off in this … um. Here's your chips.'

He trailed off, realising he should avoid dissing his job while on the floor.

The first few hands were purposely played in a casual fashion; it was time to settle in and survey the scene before getting serious. I exchanged a few nods and greetings with my fellow punters around the table and sipped on my tequila sunrise as I relaxed into the chair. A convivial table always helped to establish the feeling that it was *us*, as a group, versus the house.

Alex had decided he would remain standing and silent, still watching my back.

Our conspicuous arrival at the table had not gone unnoticed by the burly, eagle-eyed pit boss who marched over to investigate these strange new specimens.

'Good evening, gentlemen. Love the outfits. Where you from?' the pit boss enquired in a friendly but slightly puzzled manner.

'We from Sath Efrica.'

'So, you guys here on vacation, or …?'

'Nah, we here on business. We are diamond merchants. There's a conference over at Cable Beach.'

I had no idea where that came from, but he seemed to swallow it for the time being.

'Oh, that's ... interesting. Enjoy your game!'

'Thenks!'

I looked to play normally and even a little loosely until the next shoe change and tried to get into the rhythm of the table and avoid arousing suspicion. I tried to imagine what was going through the pit boss's mind—were these two eccentric South African businessmen on a working holiday, or maybe professional gamblers in disguise trying to distract his attention from the actual card play?

But most likely he simply saw right through us—just a couple of whacky mates having a fun night out.

Fortunately, the pit boss took a step back and observed from a distance, which let me get into a better groove. It would have been difficult counting the cards while trying to fend off his attention. I honed my concentration and kept a low profile for a little while until the new deck was up and the count was on. As the deck diminished, the count would become more accurate with each round. The count started to lean in our favour at +4, although my accuracy was unlikely to be spot on. Still, now it was getting time to start upping the ante in anticipation of some winning hands.

Alex continued with his stoic persona and only spoke when we needed a drink refill.

Next hand, I quadrupled the bet. The dealer was showing a five, to my jack and eight, and the positive count suggested a good chance he would go bust. He revealed his undercard, which was a seven, so he was compelled to draw another with his total of twelve. And lo, he flipped a nice king to send himself bust.

Was this the start of something big?

The count remained in our favour, so I persisted with even larger bets. Much to my delight, the next few hands went according to plan, and we raked in a decent profit before the end of the deck. I continued with the same strategy, but the next half hour was rather dull play, and I probably just broke even for that period.

I could see that the pit boss was still intrigued and keeping half an eye on us.

We weren't planning on doing this all night, so I decided I would go for it big-time when the count next became favourable. *So, here we go,* I thought to myself.

Before long, the count started to climb, and when it reached +5, I sneaked on a sizeable ante.

Ja! I hit blackjack, twenty-one.

A few of the other punters around the table were also doing quite well, and the atmosphere had become one of good team spirit and camaraderie, with each player receiving friendly congratulations for a winning hand.

Again, I went even bigger. Quite massive.

The dealer showed a six to my pair of sevens. The other players leaned in and began to take interest with raised eyebrows and excited murmurs. Mr Burly Pit Boss (BPB) decided it was time to return to the fray and see what was going on.

Alex gave me a nudge, which confirmed my instinct that this could be the chance to make a sweep. I called a split, doubled my already towering stack of chips, and played the two sevens as separate hands. My palms became sweaty, and a shiver went down my spine. This was not going to break any bank either way, but within our little world, it was becoming quite exciting.

The dealer acknowledged the split and pulled the next card from the shoe.

It was a beautiful Queen of Hearts. *Ja!*

'I'll stick on that nice looking siventeen, thenks,' I advised the dealer.

'Okay, stay on seventeen,' he repeated to the expectant crowd.

My next card showed up—it was a dull six. My total of thirteen for this hand was in no-man's land, but with the count now strongly positive, the chances of the dealer busting out enabled me to stick on this paltry total.

'Ach, thirteen,' I cried, sounding dismayed. The table let out a sigh in unison.

'But you know what? In Sath Efrica, thirteen is *lekker*! I'll stick on thet!'

I waved my hand over the cards, indicating I was indeed standing pat.

This raised multiple gasps from around the table. Was I crazy?

Mr BPB broke into half a knowing grin. It appeared that he now realised what I'd been up to. I could also tell from his relaxed expression that he also understood that I wasn't exactly going to bring the house down, and maybe he appreciated that at least we'd brought a bit of excitement and more punters to his table.

The dealer cleared his throat. 'That's a stay on thirteen, right?'

'Ebsolutely!' I replied with gusto.

The crowd hushed as next card was slowly pulled from the shoe with dramatic effect.

Our young dealer slowly turned it over to reveal the lovely ten of diamonds. *How beautifully appropriate,* I thought. *Diamonds are indeed forever.* So, the house held a miserable sixteen and was on the brink of defeat.

My heart skipped a beat as the last card came forth. It was turned over and revealed,

'It's a six!'

The house was busted.

'*Ja*, sex!' I screamed. 'I love that sex!'

The table laughed and hollered along with us as I raked in the big pile of clanking chips.

Alex broke out of his zombie state and high-fived each and every person in the small crowd that had gathered. We were jubilant, not just because we'd succeeded in our blackjack masterplan but because it had been a whole lot of fun too.

As we made to leave the table and cash in our winnings, I rolled a fifty-dollar chip across the table to our tiring Mancunian friend.

'Thenks for the game, dude! Here's a tip—enjoy!'

'Ooh, cheers cock!'

But before we got to leave the scene, Mr Burly Pit Boss made his way around the table and reached into his pocket, pulling out some pieces of paper, which he waved in our direction.

'It's been very interesting hosting you guys this evening. Here's a couple of vouchers for a complimentary dinner at the Paradise Restaurant. I hope to see you again later.'

'Oh, *ja*, thenks my friend,' I replied gratefully. '*Ja*, we'll ketch you later on!'

The concept of a 'comp' was not lost on me. Its design is to bring people back to the tables at some point, giving the house an opportunity to win back more than they might have lost initially.

Still, it was a nice gesture, but that would be the last they'd see of us!

Alex and I enjoyed a satisfying meal at the Paradise Restaurant, and we then pondered on what to do next. It had been an exciting few hours at the casino, and we were a bit drained after maintaining those bizarre personas for an extended period.

'So, let's see. What are the options. How about Goombay?' Alex began.

Goombay Beach Club was the local haunt of many of the ship's staff and crew, who partied on the beach to the sound of local reggae and calypso bands up until the ship sailed at 5 am.

'Hmm. Not sure. It'll be full of people from the ship,' I replied.

'Yeah, you're right; it might be more fun to stay incognito. Let's go somewhere different—what about Waterloo? We haven't been there in ages.'

So, the scene was set for our next trip into the unknown. The Waterloo Club was a sprawling outdoor nightclub on the main island, a former lakeside colonial mansion not far from Paradise Casino. It was mostly frequented by young Americans on vacation, some of the ship's passengers, and was also popular with the Nassau locals on the weekend. We'd only been there a couple of times before.

Our accommodating taxi driver helped us score some weed on the way, so by the time we arrived at Waterloo, we felt fully loaded and ready for more action. Drugs weren't a big thing in our lives; for us, it was just an occasional dabble on a special night. The nightclub was heaving, so we edged our way to the bar through the throngs of dancing partygoers. The subdued lighting in the main bar area meant that we went largely unnoticed, so we ordered a couple of margaritas and wandered around the club as the music pumped.

The outdoor area was bustling with US college students in party mode on Spring Break. A beautifully lit turquoise ten-metre swimming pool took centre stage, surrounded by a dozen tall, white Grecian columns and flowering bushes marking out the perimeter of a sizeable patio area.

Then suddenly it was apparent that the bright lighting meant our unusual appearance was no longer invisible.

'Hey, look at these guys!' exclaimed one young party animal, clutching his beer and thrusting it in our direction. His group of friends spun around and welcomed us over to join them while clocking our unusual get-up.

'Whoa! What's happening, man!'

'Hey, dudes!'

Alex and I sauntered over to greet them.

'Hello! Nice to meet you all! Looks like you're all having a good time here,' said Alex enthusiastically, having slipped back into to his normal friendly personality. We shook hands and clinked glasses with the various guys and girls of the group.

'Yeah, we're having a blast! It's awesome here,' the leader of the pack shouted, holding both arms aloft and reaching for the stars with his ever-spilling beer bottle.

'So where are you from?' I asked.

'South Carolina,' they answered together. 'We're all at college in Columbia.'

'But hold on, y'all have a kinda weird accent!' figured one of the girls.

'Yeah—are you English?' interjected her friend.

Alex replied, 'Ah, yes. Well spotted. I'm from Manchester.'

'So, what are you guys doing here—y'all look like … um …'

And then my addled brain began to play tricks again as a flurry of wild ideas came in from left field.

'We're in the rock band Inspiral Carpets,' I calmly explained. 'We're over here recording an album, just down the road at Compass Point Studios.'

I glanced across to Alex, who was clearly trying to deadpan this startling new information.

'Wow, really!' came the excited reply from our new friends. 'That's so cool!'

'Yeah. This is Alex; he's on guitar. And I'm Dave, the drummer!'

The Manchester music scene had exploded in the previous few years; a combination of indie-pop, acid house, and psychedelia had transformed into a collection of chart-topping bands such as The Happy Mondays, Inspiral Carpets, and Stone Roses. The new phenomenon became widely known as 'Madchester'.

Having spent six months working in a Manchester hospital before my job in Bristol, I was familiar with some of the current goings-on in that northern English city. However, I had been studying for my surgical exams during that time, so barring a few visits to the well-known Hacienda and Brickhouse clubs, I didn't really get much chance to experience the Madchester revolution firsthand.

Except maybe for one memorable house party that I hosted towards the end of that job.

The invite read:

Wear your flares, platform shoes.
Thermal underwear in various hues.
Fuck-off collars, fuck-off ties.
Never mind the quality, feel the size.
Bad Taste City is where it's at,
So come on down and dress like a twat!

The Bates Street Boys travelled the thirty miles over the Pennine mountains from Sheffield, accompanied by a bevy of our close female friends and girlfriends. The crew were all kitted out in appropriately ridiculous costumes; Guy dressed up as a drag queen (although quite appropriately, he resembled Coronation Street's Hilda Ogden rather than the glamorous RuPaul). Dirk and Pete sported Hendrix-esque sequins and bandanas, while the Tapt-Off Ladies wore stunning psychedelic catsuits with matching hair, make-up, and fake tattoos. On the drive over the winding Snake Pass, the crazy convoy came upon a car accident at an isolated spot ahead, so they stopped to help. I could only imagine the horror on the faces of the potentially injured passengers when reassuring words emanated from Guy's lipstick-smeared gob.

'It's okay—we're all doctors and nurses!'

Suitably bad-taste, medically inspired cocktails and shots were the order of the day, ranging from lime-green blobs of jelly in a crème-de-menthe-flavoured drink served in sputum pots to a pus-resembling brandy alexander delivered in laboratory test-tubes.

The cherry on the top was provided by some of the local lads from the hospital. This fine group of chefs, porters, and orderlies created my treasured Madchester Mix tape, which never left my side for years to come.

The Inspiral Carpets idea had come from nowhere and was only intended as a spontaneous bit of fun, but our drunken audience fell for it completely—hook, line, and sinker. Before we knew it, Alex and I were swept along on a magic carpet, signing autographs and having our pictures taken with our new fans around the poolside.

We continued with our outlandish story, carefully trying not to tie ourselves in knots with our revelations describing our fake musical careers and exploits. So, we bought a few rounds of drinks for all and sundry to help keep the party going, and this we did with a little guilt in our hearts from the deception. But the gesture just seemed to confirm our standing as eccentric rockstars, especially when I had to pull out the bulging wad of hundred-dollar bills at the bar.

Alex and I revelled in the spotlight for far longer than our allotted fifteen minutes of fame, dancing and cavorting our merry way around Waterloo amid the South Carolina Crowd who had taken us in as their own. But eventually the partying took its toll; we were worn out and needed some downtime. Maybe we didn't have the stamina of proper legendary rockstars, but it had indeed been a long night.

So, with hugs and kisses all round, we made our departure and hopped into a waiting cab.

'Bloody hell, I'm knackered,' Alex gasped as he slunk back into the comfort of the spacious back seat.

'Yeah. Me too,' I agreed. 'Where to next?'

'How about a quiet drink at the Drop Off?'

'Good idea. Time for a nightcap maybe.'

With that, I leant over and greeted our cab driver. 'Hey, how's your night going?'

'Pretty busy tonight. Lots of party kids around.'

'Right. Can you take us to the Drop Off Club? You know where it is?'

'Yeah, sure. No problem,' came his friendly reply.

Our cab slowly left the kerbside, and while plopping back into my seat, I glanced out of the rear window.

'Hang on a minute!' I spluttered, giving Alex a sharp whack on the arm.

Alex roused himself from his incipient slumber. 'What's going on?'

'Look! It's the Carolina Crowd. They're getting into that taxi behind us!'

'So what? Maybe they're just going home?'

But this was weird. It didn't seem likely that they had suddenly decided it was home time for them too.

As our cab began making its way down East Bay Street, I kept an eye on the taxi behind us. The Carolina cab came up close behind, then proceeded to follow our every turn.

'They're bloody following us!' I concluded, not sure if this was a good thing or not.

Alex detected the apprehension in my voice.

'Nah, don't be daft,' he rebuffed me. 'You're getting paranoid.'

'No, they are! Look! Look! They're right behind us.'

It was only a couple of miles to the Drop Off Club, so it wouldn't be difficult for them to keep up with us if I was indeed correct.

Alex wasn't convinced. 'But why would they be following us? That's nuts.'

'No idea.'

I started to try and figure out what was going on. Maybe they had just been having so much fun with a couple of rockstar dudes that they simply wanted to keep the party going?

Could be.

Or perhaps they had just realised that we were complete fakes and wanted to smash our heads in?

Holy crap!

'Here we go, boys,' announced our driver as he slowed down and pulled up outside the club.

The other taxi was still about a hundred yards behind us, and now my paranoia was taking a full hold. Alex sat bolt upright, totally alert, and was now clearly infected by my delusional thinking. He quickly pulled out a fifty-dollar bill and slapped it down on the console.

'Thanks, mate. Keep the change.'

We both made a rapid exit and bolted for the dark interior of the Drop Off Club, not really knowing what the hell was going on. The small nightclub wasn't that busy, so we made a beeline over to the far side of the bar to evade the chasing party of groupies. From this partially hidden viewpoint, we closely watched the entrance door, nervous with anticipation.

'They're here!' Alex pointed out.

Four Carolina lads and a couple of the girls had indeed chased us across town and now entered the dimly lit arena. But what was their demeanour? Were they happy and smiling or looking to give us a good whacking?

We watched on as they slowly scanned the room, trying to locate our position, but it was too dark to tell what was on their minds. Weary and dishevelled, we were now in no mood to find out either way. The Dudes had reached the point of no return, and our paranoia was now driving all our instincts.

I gave Alex a nudge and pointed out a small side door near to our end of the room.

'Quick, let's go!'

In perfect lock step, we carefully sidled over towards the fire exit. I took a sideways glance, only to see the leader of the pack pointing over towards us.

'There they are!' he shouted to the others, who followed his call and started to jog over to intercept us.

We quickly piled through the fire exit and ran like hell into an awaiting taxi outside on the nearby street.

'Drive, just drive!' Alex demanded of the startled driver.

'Um ... okay, okay!'

Thankfully, the astute cabby put his foot down before engaging his brain, and thus we sped off into the night.

The dilapidated Dudes skulked back aboard ship, still reeling from the crazy night out. Alex rubbed his tummy.

'I'm feeling a bit peckish now. We've missed the midnight buffet—you got any food in your cabin?'

'Nah. But I think there's a stash of baked beans in the infirmary.'

'Baked beans ... really? Fantastic! The perfect cure for an attack of the munchies.'

I grabbed two cans of Heinz baked beans from the infirmary fridge and popped the contents into a couple of metal kidney bowls. We didn't have any forks either, so we had to improvise with a couple of wooden tongue depressors.

'Yum! Just what the doctor ordered,' Alex giggled as he tried to balance a few of the beans perilously on his inadequate cutlery.

'Yeah, can't beat good ol' baked beans, hey. They're sure hitting the spot.'

The emergency rations certainly fulfilled their duty, and the kidney bowls were gradually emptied, almost bean by bean.

Alex looked around the infirmary while scoffing his late-night snack, interested in all the medical equipment dotted around the room. He pointed over towards the bed.

'Hey, Paolo, what's that thing over there?'

'That's the defibrillator. You know, the thing we use to shock people back when their heart stops,' I explained.

'Ah, right. Like in *Flatliners*?'

'Yep. But that movie obviously stretched things a bit. If your heart stays stopped for more than three minutes without CPR, chances are that you'll end up brain-dead.'

'Really?'

'Yeah, for sure. But someone who's healthy would probably be okay if we got them back in a minute or two.'

Alex was clearly fascinated with this lifesaving device.

'So do people get strange dreams and stuff when they're under, like in the movie?'

'Hmm, I doubt it. That movie was pretty scary. But there are lots of stories about people who have had a near-death experience. You know, like seeing a bright light inviting them to heaven or other weird shit.'

This conversation triggered my brain into mischievous mode once again, and yet another whacky idea presented itself.

'So … shall we have a game of *Flatliners*?'

'What do you mean?' Alex asked with a curious look.

My face remained deadpan, and I made sure I spoke with the confidence of a rational doctor rather than a drunken South African diamond dealer or stoned rockstar.

'Well, I can shock your heart, so it'll stop. But then I'll get you back quickly, say, after a minute.'

Alex dropped a clump of beans on the floor and then unexpectedly replied, 'Alright. If you reckon I'll be okay.' He looked me square in the eye.

'Yes, you'll be fine,' I replied reassuringly.

I was of course surprised that Alex had taken up the offer, but I continued in a professional manner.

'And you won't feel a thing.'

Alex stood straight up and put both his hands on my shoulders, so we were toe to toe and face to face.

'Paolo, I trust you.'

'Good. I wouldn't suggest it if I thought there would be any risk. Let's do it.'

My great friend Alex took off his jacket and shirt and laid himself down on the bed. I began to set up the defibrillator, all the while thinking to myself, *Remember not to turn it on!*

I put the sticky conduction pads onto his chest, one slightly to the right of his sternum, the other near his heart's apex on the left side. It was clear that Alex had heeded my every word and trusted me completely, but he was getting a little nervous now.

I then grabbed hold the defibrillator paddles, one in each hand, and theatrically held them high up above Alex's chest.

'So, in a minute, I'm going to place these paddles onto your chest. Nothing will happen until I count to three and then press the shock buttons. Okay?'

Alex took a few deep breaths and looked up to the ceiling in an effort to focus and calm his nerves. I let him take a moment to steady himself, then slowly began to lower the paddles to his chest. Just as the electrodes were approaching contact with the pads, Alex suddenly put his arms up towards me, and his whole body quivered.

'Hang on, hang on!' he spluttered dramatically.

'Okay. I'll stop,' I calmly replied and withdrew the paddles of doom.

'It's okay. Just getting a bit nervous. Gimme a minute.'

My volunteer patient took a few more deep breaths and relaxed a little, continuing to set his eyes on a point above the bed.

'I'm okay now. Go for it.'

Silently, I lowered the shockers once again, and this time Alex remained calm and steady as I carefully placed them onto the pads on his chest.

I started the count.

'*One.*'

Alex's gaze shifted from the ceiling to look directly at me, his nerves now holding firm.

'*Two.*'

He braced himself, his body stiffening, with the piercing, wide-eyed glare of a man who thought he might be about to die.

Suddenly, images from my roller-coaster thirteen months in the Caribbean flashed before my eyes: the battle with Gambino, my romantic American odyssey, the magnificent Dr Mo, and the crazy things I'd witnessed and been a part of.

Plus, the great friendship I had forged with Alex the Cockroach-Killer.

How lucky I'd been.

I briefly agonised for one last time, hoping to hell I hadn't turned on the defibrillator.

'*Three!*'

—- THE END —-

CPSIA information can be obtained
at www.ICGtesting.com
Printed in the USA
BVHW031225121022
649280BV00011B/190

9 781922 854773